Contents

	Welcome to Class	2
1	Good Morning, Class!	6
2	My Family	20
3	My Body	34
Checkpoint	Units 1–3	48
4	My Favorite Clothes	50
5	Busy at Home	64
6	On the Farm	78
Checkpoint	Units 4–6	92
7	Party Time	94
8	Fun and Games	108
9	Play Time	122
Checkpoint	Units 7–9	136
	Extra Grammar Practice	138
	My Big English World	147

Welcome to Class!

1 Look, read, and match.

a Hello, I'm Patrick.

b Hello, I'm Jane.

c Hello, I'm Maria.

2 Draw and write.

What's your name?

Hello, I'm _____.

3 Look and circle.

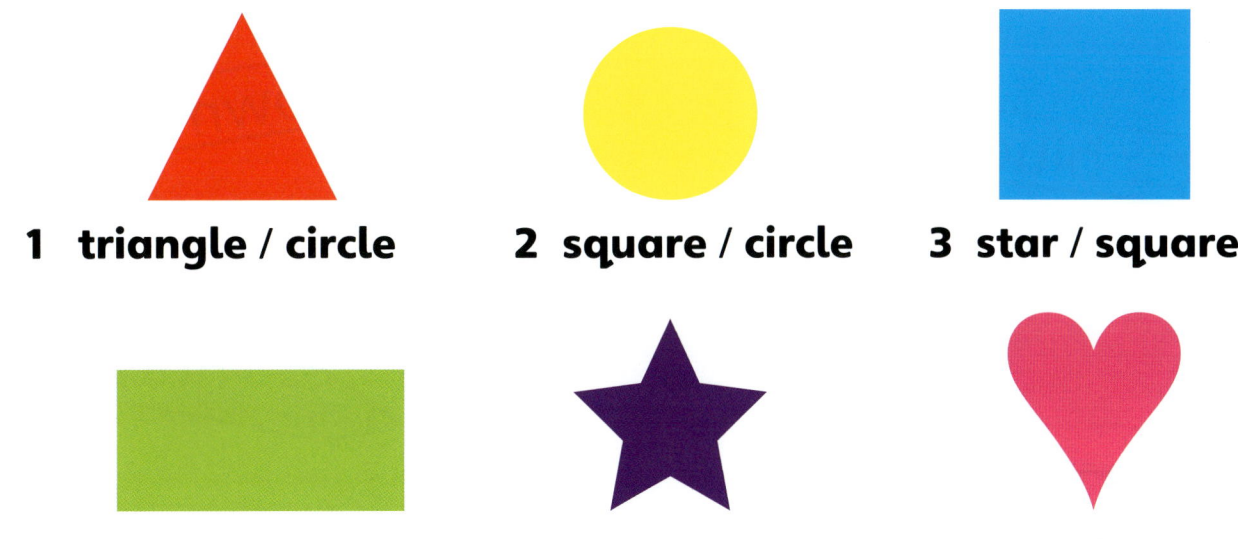

1 triangle / circle   2 square / circle   3 star / square

4 rectangle / triangle   5 star / rectangle   6 star / heart

4 Read and draw.

1 It's a triangle.   2 It's a star.   3 It's a heart.

5 **Read and color.**

6 **Color and write.**

My favorite color is _____.

7 **Read and match.**

one
two
three
four
five
six
seven
eight

nine
ten
eleven
twelve
thirteen
fourteen
fifteen

8 **Connect the dots. Write.**

It's a _____.

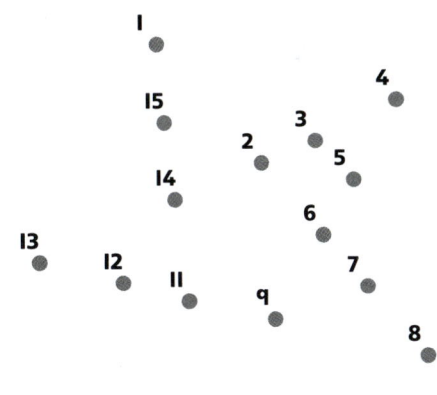

9 **Draw and write. How old are you?**

I'm _____.

Good Morning, Class!

1 **Match, color, and say.**

1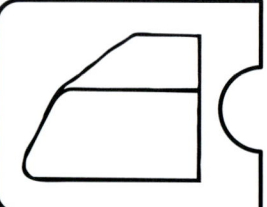

2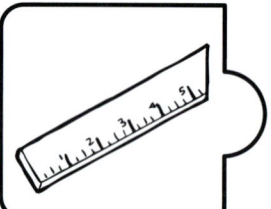

3

4

a  book

b 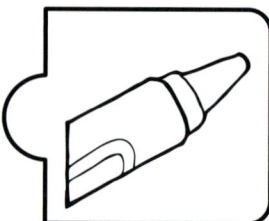 crayon

c 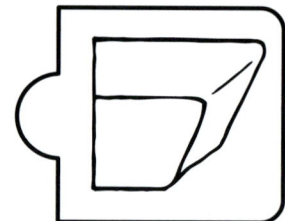 eraser

d 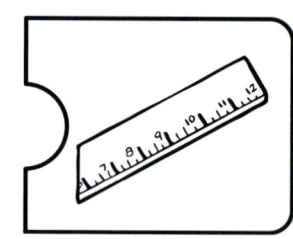 ruler

2 **Look and circle.**

1 What is it?
It's a **pen** / **marker**.

2 What is it?
It's a **backpack** / **desk**.

6   Unit 1

3. Listen and sing. Then draw.

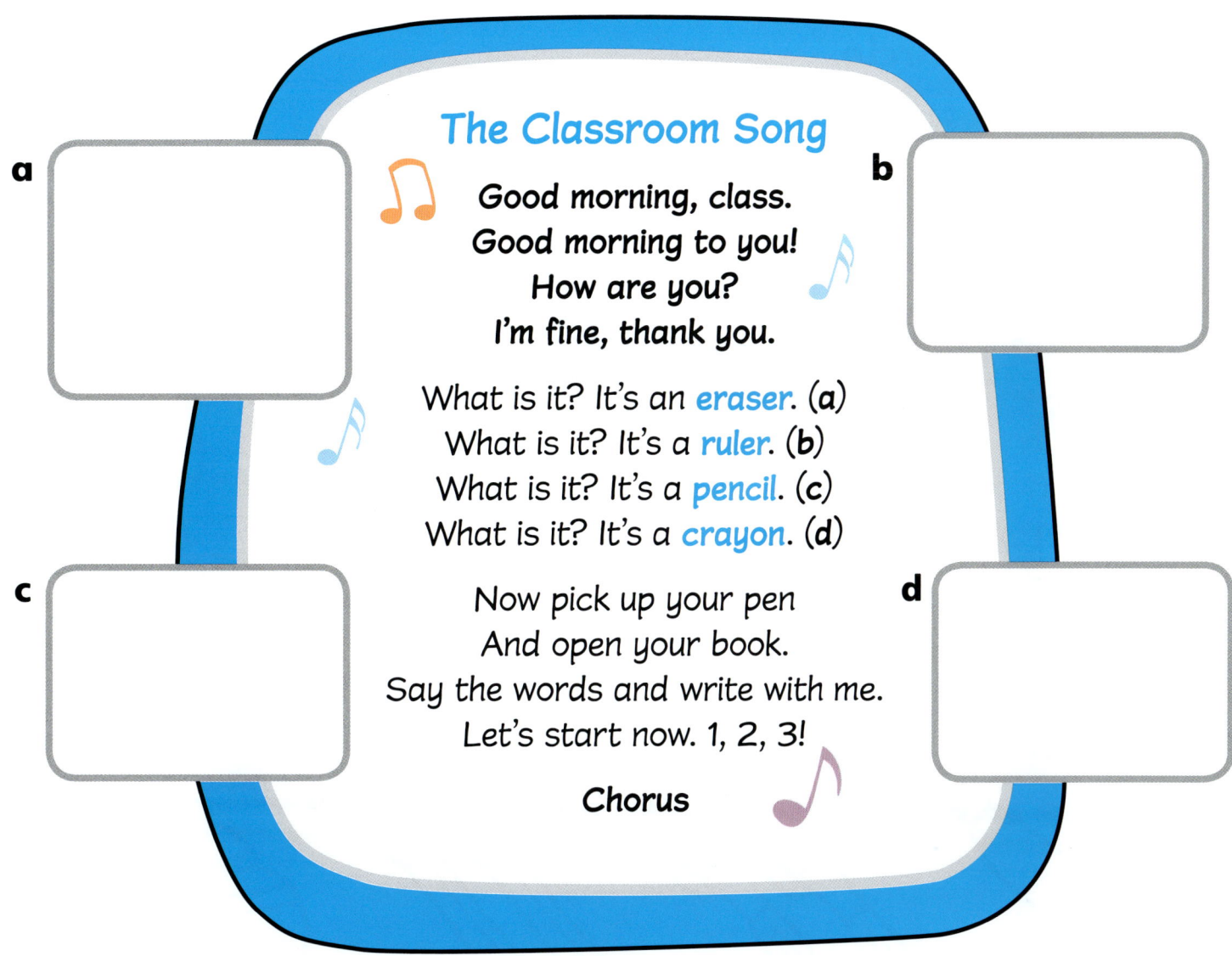

The Classroom Song

Good morning, class.
Good morning to you!
How are you?
I'm fine, thank you.

What is it? It's an eraser. (a)
What is it? It's a ruler. (b)
What is it? It's a pencil. (c)
What is it? It's a crayon. (d)

Now pick up your pen
And open your book.
Say the words and write with me.
Let's start now. 1, 2, 3!

Chorus

4. Draw your backpack. Then write.

This is my _____.
It's _____.

Unit 1   7

Story

5 Read and circle.

6 Listen and color.

1 2 3 4

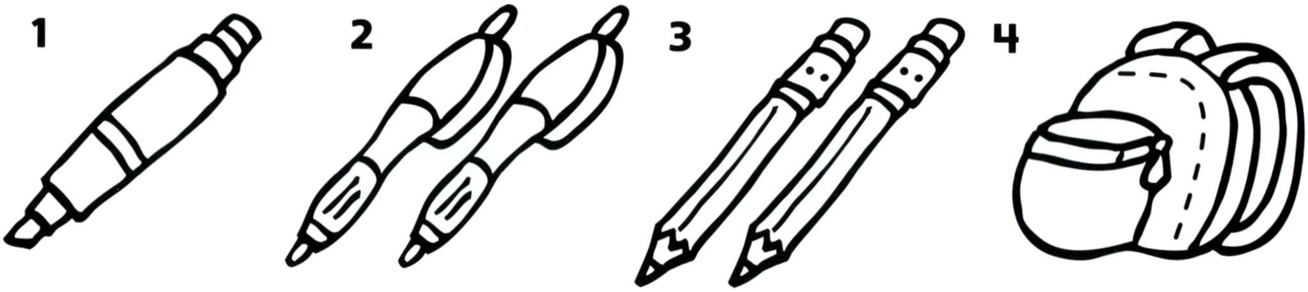

Complete the sequence.

THINK BIG   1   2   3   4

8   Unit 1

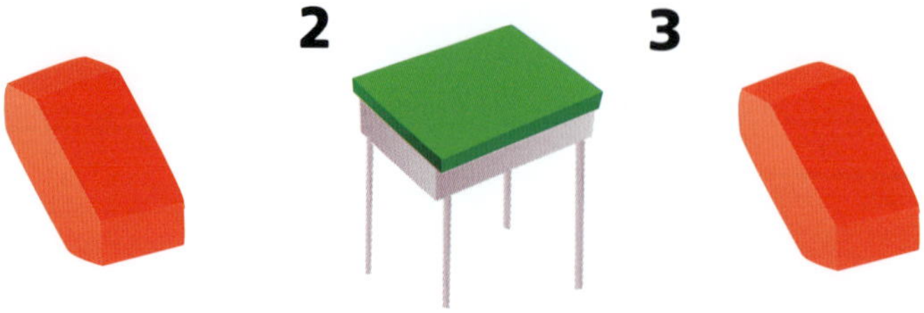

Language in Action

 7 **Listen and** **.**

1 a  ☐   b  ☐

2 a  ☐   b  ☐

3 a 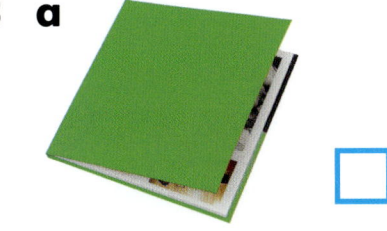 ☐   b  ☐

4 a  ☐   b  ☐

8 **Read, draw, and color.**

1 It's a pencil. It's green.

2 It's a book. It's blue.

3 It's a crayon. It's yellow.

Language in Action

What are they?

They're...

9 **Match and say.**

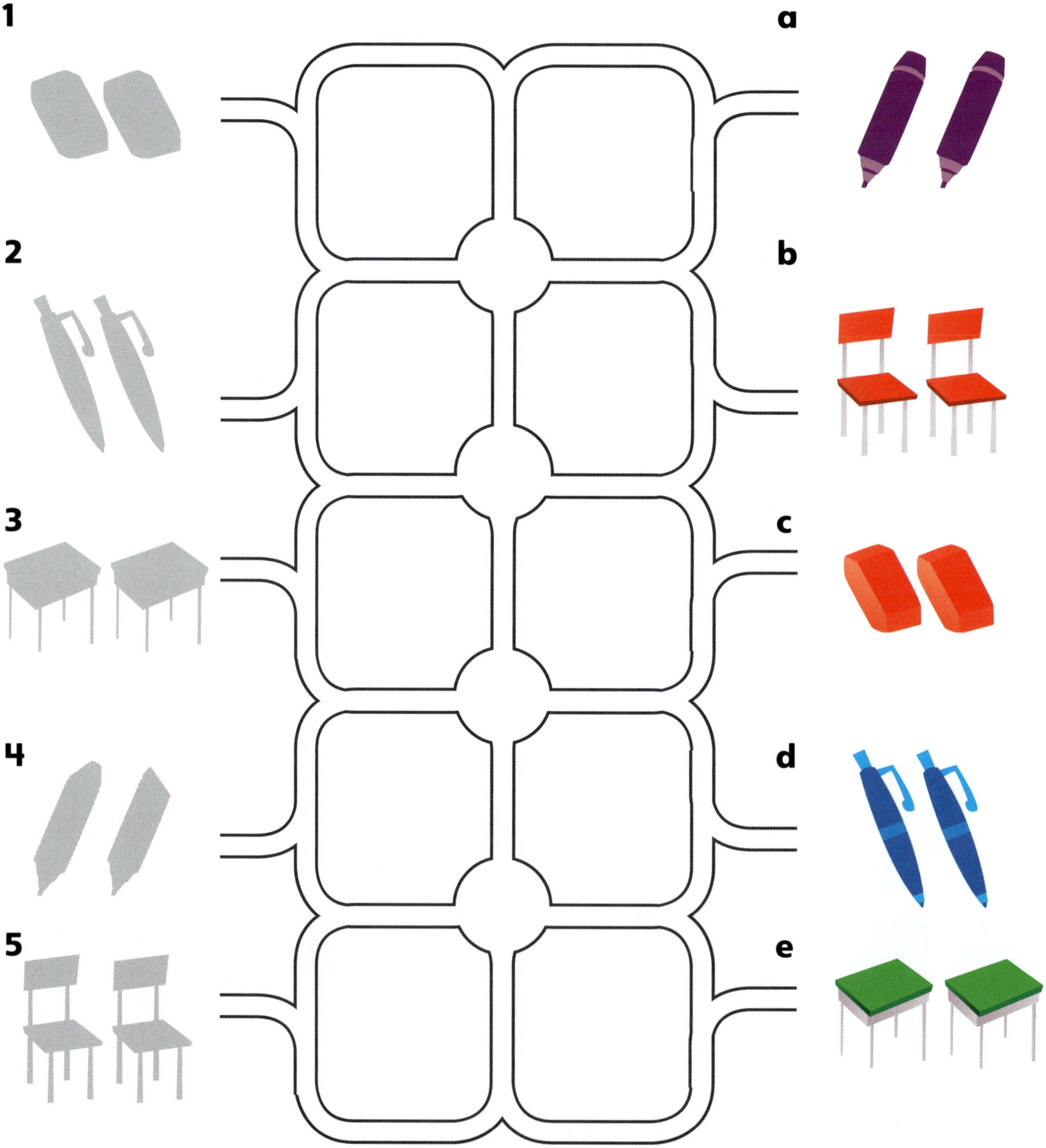

1
2
3
4
5

a
b
c
d
e

Math | Content Connection

 Look at the pictures. Then listen, read, and circle.

1 It's a **pencil case / pencil sharpener**. It's blue, red, pink, yellow, and green.

2 It's a **notebook / tablet**. It's black and white.

3 It's a **pencil / pencil sharpener**. It's red.

4 It's a **tablet / notebook**. It's green.

Count and write.

1  ____ erasers

2 ____ markers

3 ____ rulers

4  ____ desk

 I have 3 green pens and 1 red pen. How many pens do I have?
I have ____ pens.

Unit 1   11

12 Connect numbers 1 to 10. Count and write.

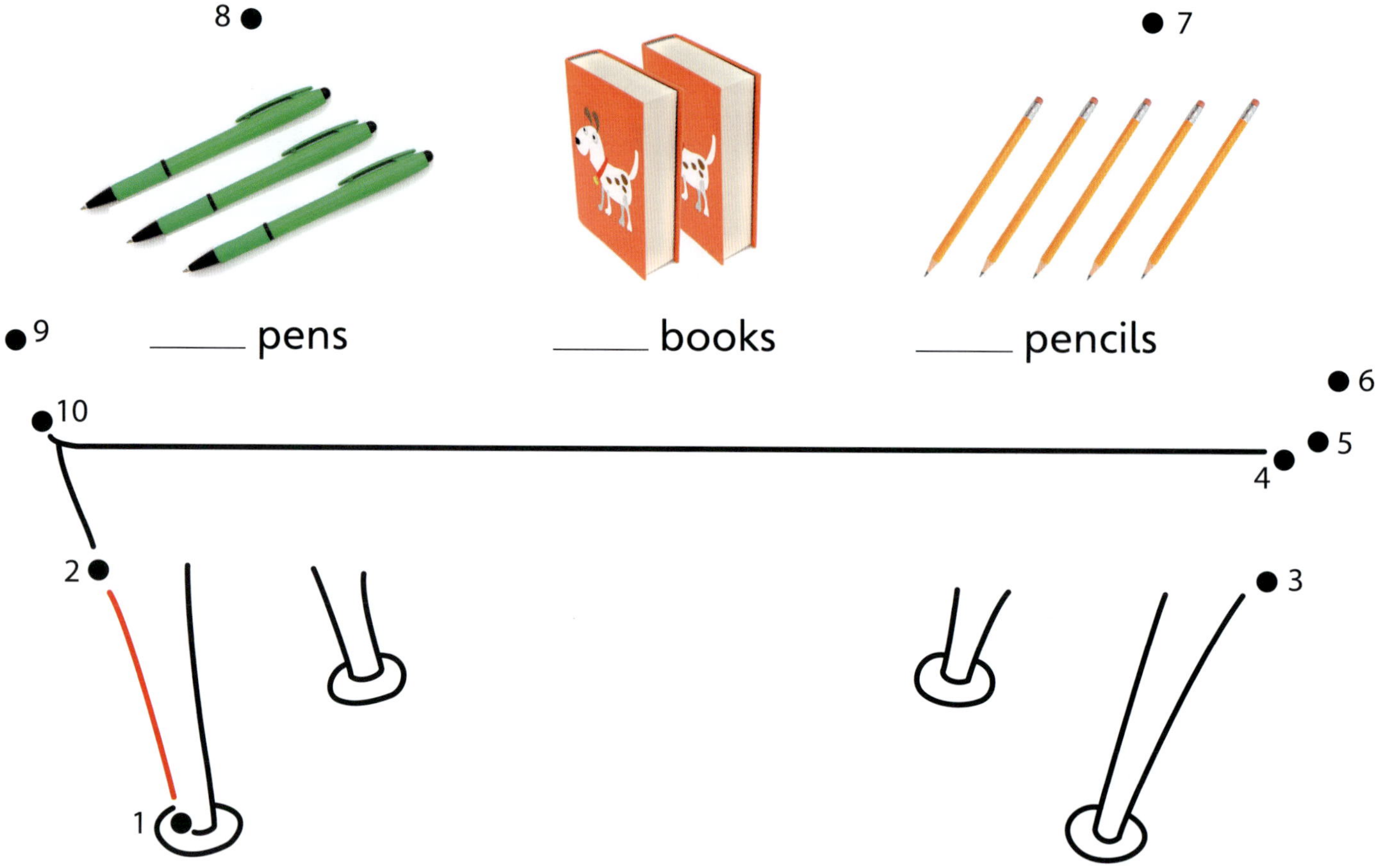

_____ pens _____ books _____ pencils

13 Look at 12. Read and circle T for true and F for false.

1 I have four green pens.   T   F
2 I have two books.   T   F
3 My pencils are red.   T   F

14 Look and write.

| pencils   sharpener   three |

1 I have two _____.
2 My pencil _____ is red.
3 I have _____ crayons.

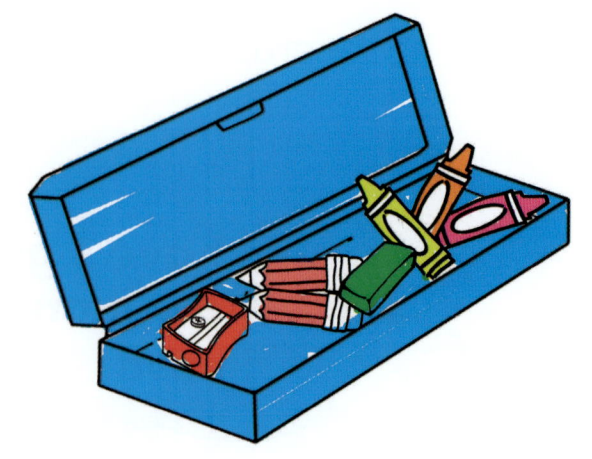

Grammar

15 **Look and write.**

> Don't eat!   Don't talk!   Look!   Sit down!

1 _____

2 _____

3 _____

4 _____

16 **Read and circle.**

1 **Stand** / **Sit** down.
2 Don't **stand** / **sit** up!
3 **Write** / **Close** your books.
4 Don't **say** / **eat** in class!
5 **Open** / **Write** your name.
6 **Say** / **Talk** the alphabet.

Culture Connection | Around the World

17 **Look and circle.**

1

2

3

1 Africa / China
2 The United States of America / Africa
3 China / Africa

18 **Listen, read, and write.**

black   gray   rulers   tablet

1 Hello! I'm Jabu. I'm seven. In Africa, my classroom is small. I have a small desk, too. My backpack is _____.

2 Hi! I'm Katie. I'm six. In the U.S.A., I have a big classroom. My desk is big and white. My favorite color is white. I have a _____, too.

3 Hello! My name is Li. I'm from China. In my classroom, I have many books, pencils, crayons, and _____. I have a small _____ tablet.

19 Look at 18. Read and circle **T** for true and **F** for false.

1 Jabu has a small classroom.   T   F
2 Katie is seven.   T   F
3 Li is from China.   T   F
4 Katie has a brown desk.   T   F
5 Jabu has a black backpack.   T   F
6 Li has a big tablet.   T   F

20 What do you have? Circle for you.

crayons   a pink eraser

a small desk   a pink backpack

           a blue pen

a big classroom
                           a small classroom

a notebook   a big desk

      a black pen   a red pen

                  a blue backpack
markers
                                a tablet
      a white eraser

THINK BIG   Look at **20**. Draw your things.

Unit 1 15

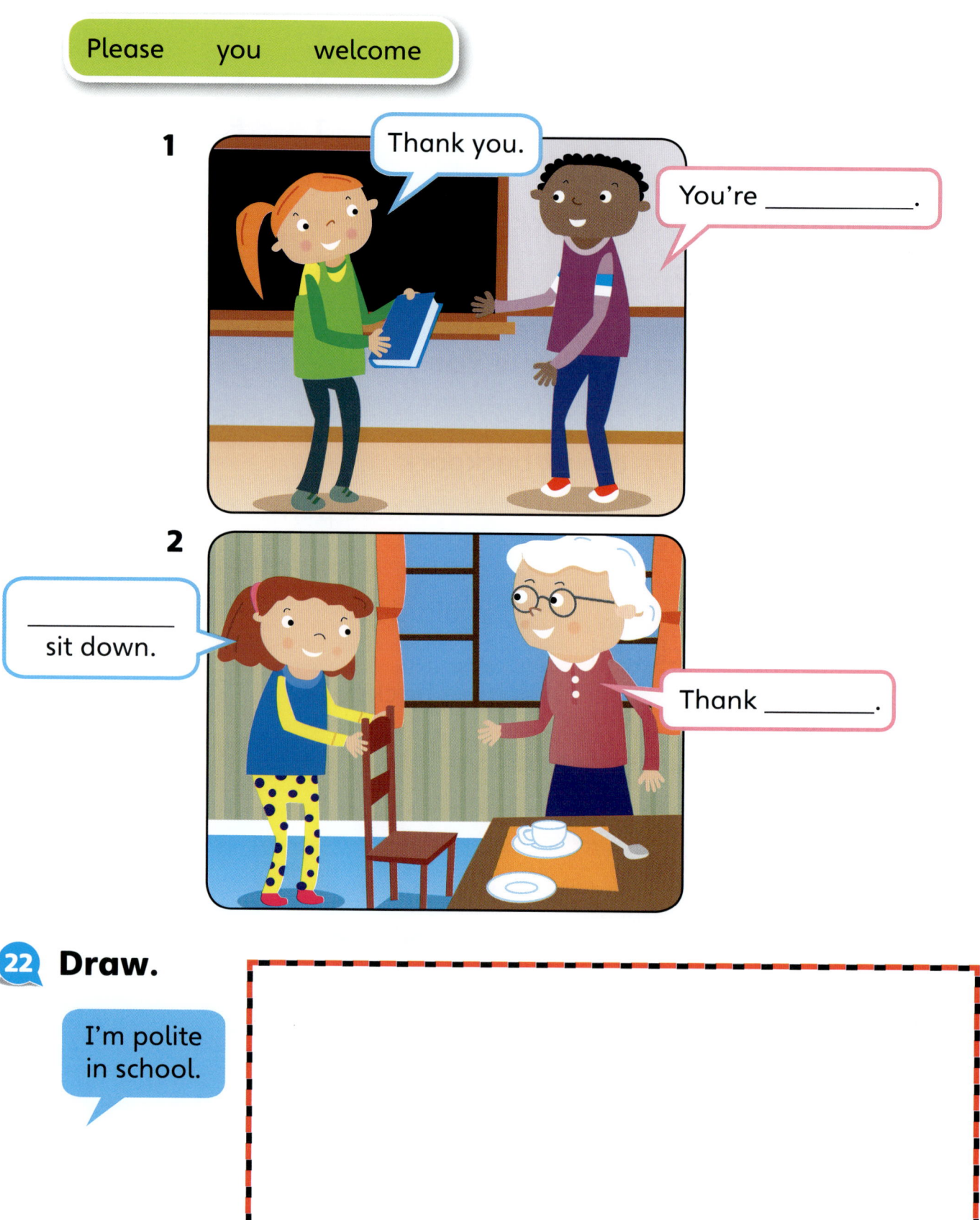

a, t, p, n | Phonics

23 Find and circle the letters **a**, **t**, **p**, and **n**.

24 Read and circle the letters **a**, **t**, **p**, and **n**.

1. and   2. ten   3. pen   4. nip

25 Match the words to the same sounds.

1 nap   a pen
2 pan   b and
3 ant   c nip

26 Listen and chant.

Pat the ant
Has a tan.
Pat the ant
Takes a nap.

Review

27 Read, draw, and color.

1 I have a pencil. It's yellow.

2 I have a desk. It's blue.

3 I have three markers. They're red.

4 I have two books. They're green.

28 Read and circle.

1 What is it?
   It's / **They're** a tablet.

2 What are they?
   It's / **They're** notebooks.

3 What is it? It's a **pencil case** / **pencil sharpener**.

4 What **is it** / **are they**? They're pencil sharpeners.

29 Read and match.

1 Don't run   a your homework.
2 Listen   b on the desk.
3 Don't write   c to your teacher.
4 Do   d in class.

Review

30 **Color.**

1 = red   2 = blue   3 = green   4 = yellow

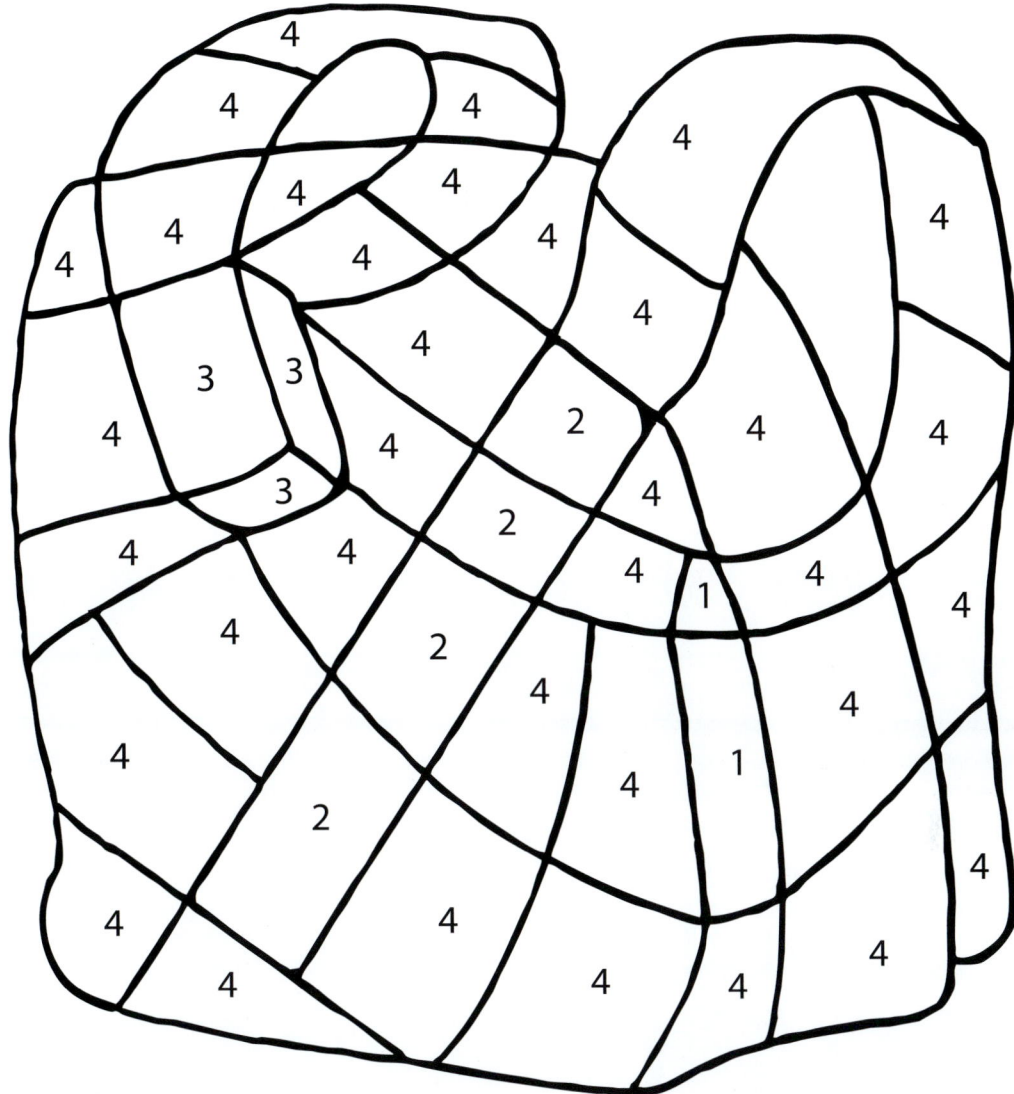

31 **Look at 30. Match.**

1 What is it? It's red.
2 What is it? It's blue.
3 What is it? It's green.
4 What is it? It's yellow.

a It's an eraser.
b It's a backpack.
c It's a crayon.
d It's a ruler.

My Family

1 Read and match.

grandma

sister

grandpa

My family.

dad

brother

mom

2 Listen and circle. Then sing.

My Family

My family, my family!
This is my family.
He's my brother / sister
And she's my brother / sister.

My dad / mom, my dad / mom!
My sister, my brother!
We have so much fun!
I love them!

My family, my family.
I love my family!
I love them, and they love me.
I love my family!

3 Draw your mom and dad. Then write.

My _____   My _____

Unit 2

Story

4 Read and point. Then read and circle.

I have...

a one brother and two sisters.
b one brother and one sister.
c two brothers and one sister.

THINK BIG

Look at 4. Check (✓) Tim's family.

Language in Action

5 **Listen and write the number.**

Language in Action

6 Read. Count and color.

24 Unit 2

Social Science | Content Connection

7 Look, read, and match.

1  2  3  4

a boy   **b** man   **c** woman   **d** girl

8 Look at the picture. Then listen, read, and circle.

This is my family.

I am a ¹**boy / girl.** My name's Ian.

This ²**man / boy** is my dad. This ³**girl / woman** is my mom.

This ⁴**boy / baby** is my brother. This ⁵**girl / boy** is my sister.

This ⁶**girl / woman** is my grandma, and this is my grandpa.

THINK BIG

Are you a boy or a girl?

I'm a _____.

Unit 2

9 **Look, read, and match.**

1 This woman is my grandma.

2 This girl is my sister.

3 This woman is my mom.

4 This man is my grandpa.

5 This boy is my brother.

a
b
c
d
e

10 **Look and write.**

boy   girl (x2)   man (x2)   woman (x2)

Grammar

11 🎧 58 **Listen and ✓.**

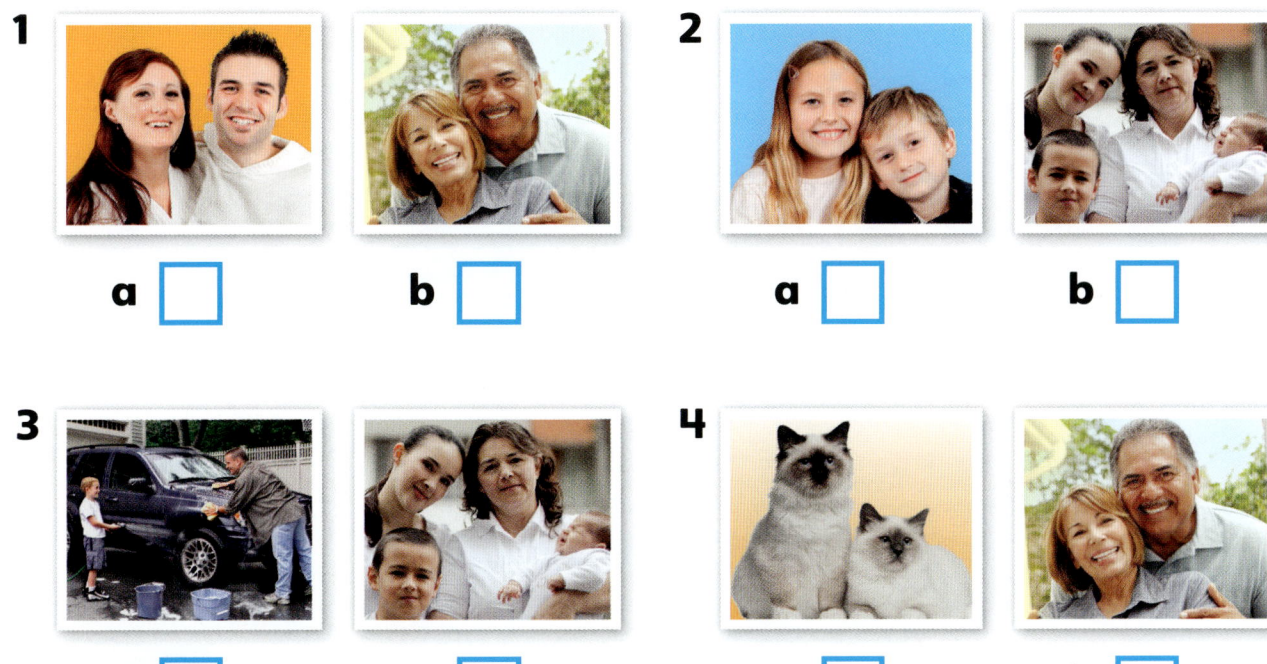

12 **Read and circle.**

1 This is my **brother** / **sisters**.

2 These are my **grandma** / **brothers**.

3 This is my **grandparents** / **grandpa**.

4 These are my **parents** / **baby brother**.

13 **Look, read, and match.**

1 His name's Dan.

2 Her name's Amy.

Culture Connection | Around the World

14 Look and write. Who are they?

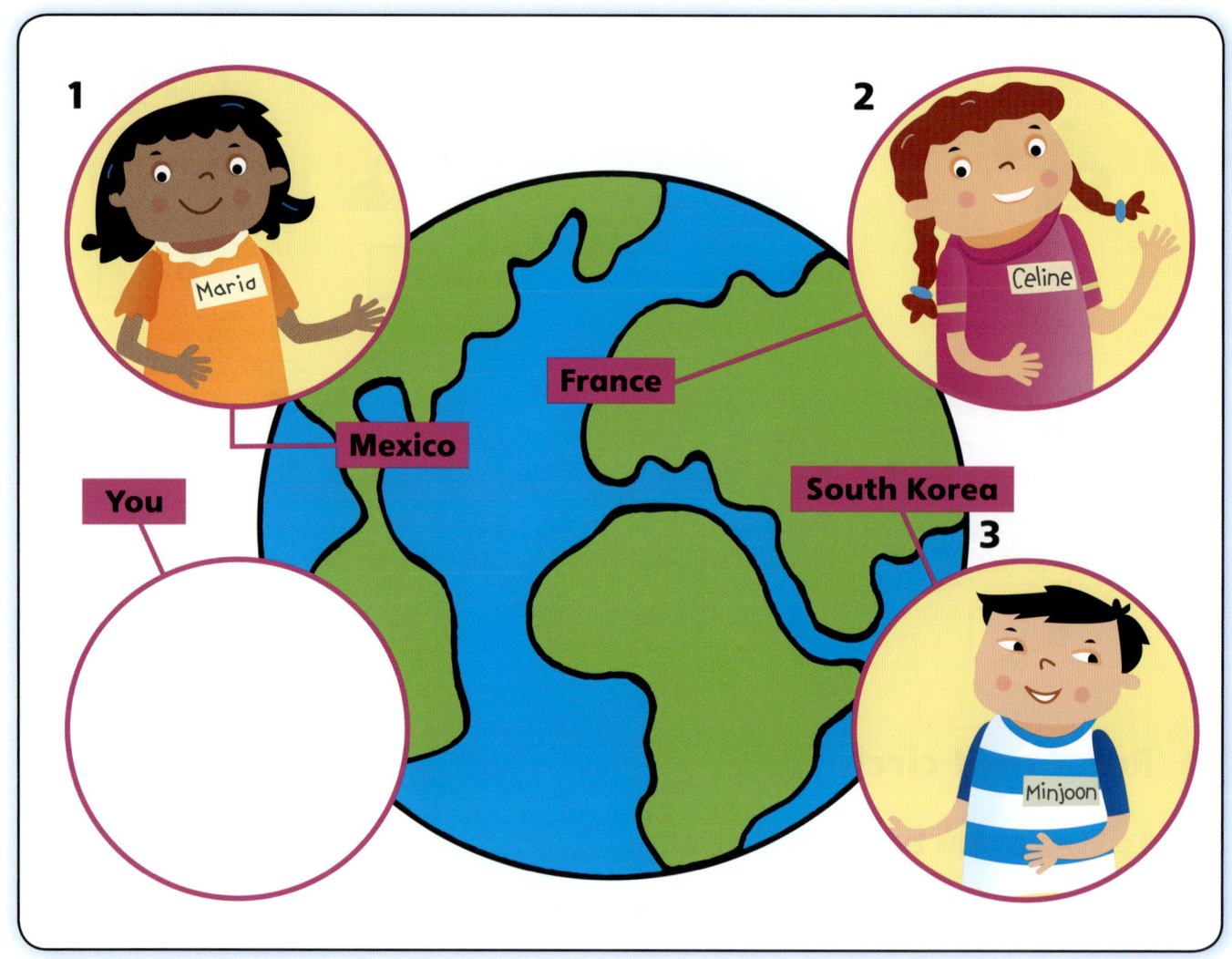

1 Her name's _____. She's from Mexico.

2 Her name's _____. She's from France.

3 His name's _____. He's from South Korea.

15 Look at **14** and draw. What's your name? Where are you from?

My name's _____. I'm from _____.

16 Listen, read, and circle.

This is my family, and these are my friends. Maria is a **¹girl / friend**. She's my **²sister / best friend**. Minjoon is a **³family / boy**. He's my friend, too. This is my **⁴sister / friend**. Her name's Celine. I love my **⁵family / sister** and friends!

17 Look at 16. Read and circle T for true and F for false.

1. Maria is a boy. T F
2. Minjoon is a girl. T F
3. Maria is my best friend. T F
4. Celine is my brother. T F
5. I love my family and friends. T F

18 Find and write the words.

1. _____ steb ndeirf
2. _____ dsreinf
3. _____ ylmaif

THINK BIG

Draw your best friend's family.

Values | Help your family.

19 **Listen and match.**

1

a Tommy helps his mom.   b Pam helps her brother.

2

20 **Draw.**

I can help!

i, s, b, d | Phonics

21 Find and circle the letters **i**, **s**, **b**, and **d**.

22 Read and circle the letters **i**, **s**, **b**, and **d**.

1. dad   2. in   3. bat   4. sit

23 Match the words with the same sounds.

1 dad   a sad
2 in   b dip
3 sit   c it

24 Listen and chant.

Don't sit, sit, sit
On a pin, pin, pin
It's bad, bad, bad
To sit on a pin!

Unit 2 31

Review

25 **Find the family words. Color them green.**

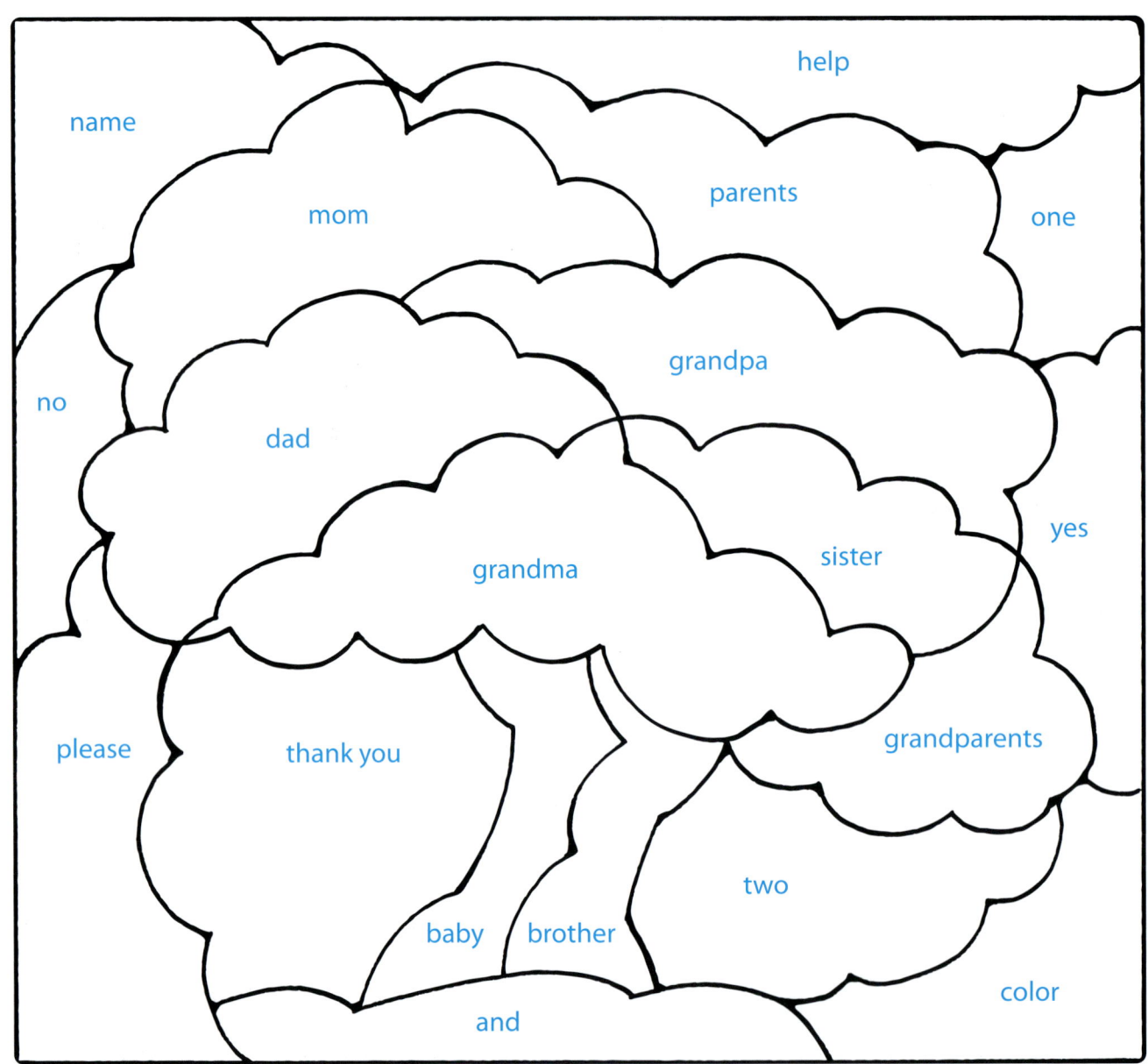

26 **Read and match.**

                        my parents.

This is   my family.

These are   my friends.

                        my best friend.

Review

27 Look and match. Then read.

1   **a** man

2  **b** girl

3  **c** boy

4  **d** woman

28 Draw your family. Then say.

This is my family.

My Body

1 Read and match.

eye — head

nose — ear

neck — mouth

leg — finger

hand — arm

toe — foot

2 Draw your friend.

3. Listen and circle. Then sing.

My Body Song

Do you have two eyes / ears?
Do you have one mouth / nose?
Do you have two eyes?
Yes, I do. Yes, I do.

I have ten fingers / toes.
I have ten toes.
I have two hands / feet
And one big nose!

And do you have long hair / legs?
And do you have short hair / arms?
And do you have small hands?
I sing my body song, my body song,
I sing my body song again!

4. Read and write.

| one | ten | ten | two | two |

1 I have _____ fingers.

2 I have _____ nose.

3 I have _____ toes.

4 I have _____ ears.

5 I have _____ eyes.

Unit 3 35

Story

5 **Read and match.**

a Yes, he does! Bobo has one eye!

b No. My teddy bear has small ears.

Brown? Oh! Does he have one eye?

Is this your teddy bear?

6 **Read and circle Yes or No.**

1 Is Bobo green? **Yes   No**
2 Does Bobo have small ears? **Yes   No**
3 Does he have long legs? **Yes   No**
4 Does he have one eye? **Yes   No**

This is _____. He's my favorite teddy bear.
He has **big / small** eyes.
He has **big / small** ears.
He has **short / long** legs.

Language in Action

7 **Read, match, and circle.**

1. Does he have long legs?
   Yes, he does. / No, he doesn't.

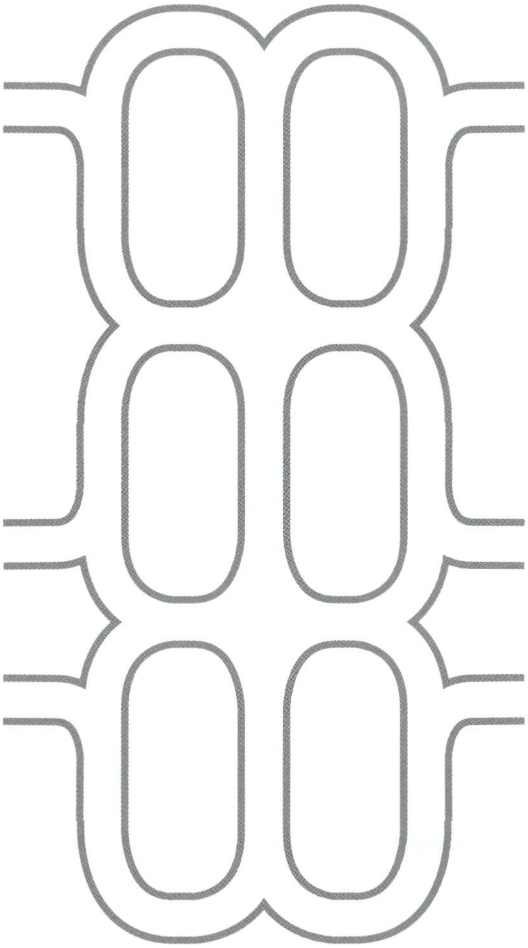

2. Does it have short ears?
   Yes, it does. / No, it doesn't.

3. Does she have long hair?
   Yes, she does. / No, she doesn't.

8

1. a   b

2. a   b

Language in Action

9 Connect numbers 1 to 10. What is it?

10 Look at 9. Circle the answer.

1  Does it have long ears? Yes, it does. / No, it doesn't.

2  Does it have small eyes? Yes, it does. / No, it doesn't.

3  Does it have a big nose? Yes, it does. / No, it doesn't.

Science | Content Connection

11 Look and circle.

1  2  3  4

see / hear   taste / smell   see / taste   hear / smell

12 Listen, read, and write.

a 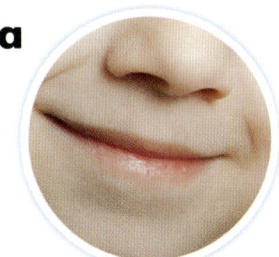 b  c 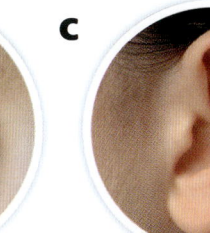 d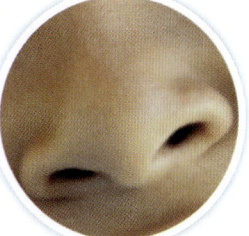

1 I hear with my ears. I hear a song. ☐

2 I see with my eyes. I see a star. ☐

3 I taste with my mouth. I taste ice cream. ☐

4 I smell with my nose. I smell flowers. ☐

I see...   I smell...   I taste...   I hear...

THINK BIG

Unit 3 39

13 Read and write.

| ears   eyes   mouth   nose |

1 I have one _____. I smell a flower.
2 I have two _____. I see a picture.
3 I have one _____. I taste cake.
4 I have two _____. I hear music.

14 Find and circle.

| ears   eyes   hear   mouth   nose   see   smell   taste |

e	a	r	s	n	n	a	q
y	z	g	m	o	u	t	h
e	n	v	e	s	l	a	e
s	e	e	l	e	c	s	a
p	b	l	l	k	d	t	r
v	d	j	m	v	g	e	x

Grammar

15 **Read and circle.**

  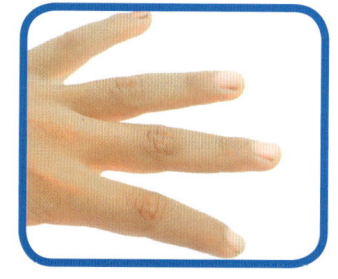

1 It's a / It's an chair.
2 It's a / It's an egg.
3 It's a / They're fingers.

16 **Complete the chart. Write It's a, It's an, and They're.**

It's a marker.	They're markers.
1 _____ triangle.	They're triangles.
2 _____ orange.	They're oranges.
It's an egg.	3 _____ eggs.

17 **Look and match.**

1 It's a   a toes.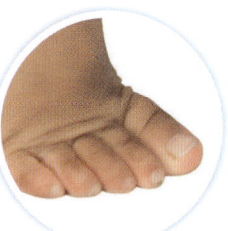

2 They're   b backpack.

3 It's an   c apple.

Unit 3   41

Culture Connection | Around the World

18 Look and match.

1 yellow   a
2 white   b
3 brown   c
4 purple   d
5 orange   e
6 black   f

19 Look at the pictures. Then listen, read, and write the colors.

| blue   green   red   yellow |

1  France has a _____, white, and red flag.

2  The flag from South Africa is _____, green, yellow, black, and white.

3  The green, _____, and blue flag is from Brazil.

4 Ireland has a _____, white, and orange flag.

20 Look at **19**. Read and circle **T** for true and **F** for false.

1. The flag from France is green, white, and red. T F
2. Ireland has an orange, white, and green flag. T F
3. The yellow, green, red, white, and black flag is from South Africa. T F
4. Brazil has a yellow, red, and green flag. T F

21 Find and write the words.

1. _____ lpruep
2. _____ earogn
3. _____ worbn
4. _____ ihetw
5. _____ llowye
6. _____ klacb

THINK BIG Draw a flag for a new country! Then write the colors.

_____
_____
_____

Unit 3 43

Values | Keep clean.

22 **Listen and match. Then sing.**

Keep Clean

1
Every day
Before I eat
And after I play
I wash my hands.

2
With a lot of soap
It's easy, you see.
Rinse with water
Just like me.

3
Dry them well and
Sing this song.
Keep your hands clean
All day long!

a

b

c

23 **Draw.**

I keep clean.

e, c, g, m | **Phonics**

24 Find and circle the letters e, c, g, and m.

25 Read and circle the letters e, c, g, and m.

1. gas   2. map   3. cap   4. pen

26 Match the words with the same sounds.

1 get   a cat
2 mat   b map
3 cap   c gas

27 Listen and chant.

The cap is on the cat.
The cat goes on the map.
The pen goes on the bed.

Unit 3 **45**

Review

28 Read and circle.

1
Does he have a long nose?
Yes, he does. / No, he doesn't.

2
Does he have small feet?
Yes, he does. / No, he doesn't.

3
Does he have short hair?
Yes, he does. / No, he doesn't.

29 Read and circle.

1 **It's a** / **It's an** nose.
2 **They're** / **It's an** ears.
3 **It's an** / **It's a** eye.
4 **It's a** / **They're** mouth.
5 **It's an** / **They're** eyes.

Review

30 Look and write.

arm
eye
finger
leg
mouth
nose

1 _____
2 _____
3 _____
4 _____
5 _____
6 _____

31 Draw and match.

This is me.

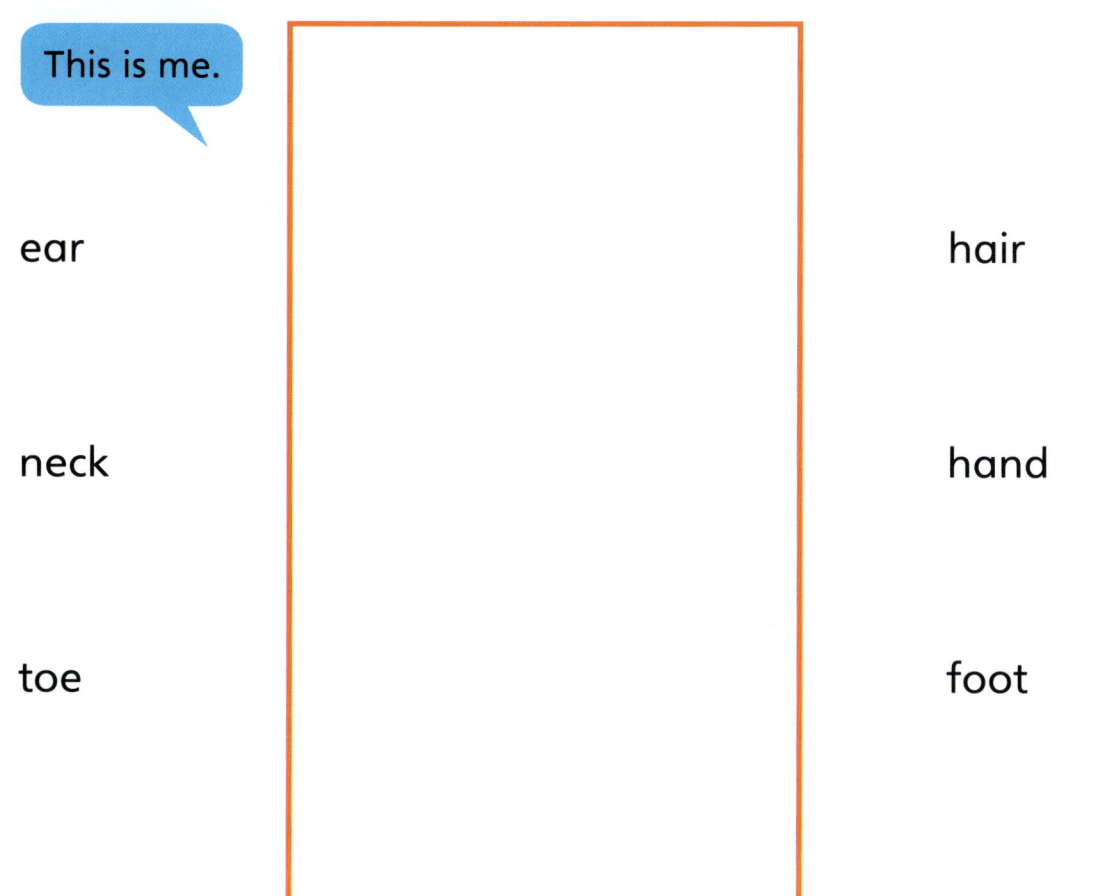

ear   hair

neck   hand

toe   foot

Unit 3 47

Checkpoint | Units 1–3

1 **Look, find, and number.**

CLASS
1 crayons
2 erasers
3 pens
4 rulers

2 **Look and ✓.**
Tom has:

My List
- [ ] pens
- [ ] pencils
- [ ] erasers
- [ ] a ruler

3 **Think and draw. Tom doesn't have:**

unit 4 My Favorite Clothes

1 Color. Then match.

a red blouse   blue pants   a yellow jacket

1 = red
2 = blue
3 = yellow

yellow boots   a blue skirt   red shoes   red gloves

2 Draw.

My Favorite Clothes

3 Listen and circle. Then chant.

What Are You Wearing?

What are you wearing?
I'm wearing a T-shirt / shirt.
What are you wearing?
I'm wearing a skirt / blouse.

What's he wearing?
He's wearing new pants / shorts.
What's he wearing?
He's wearing old shoes / boots.

What's she wearing?
She's wearing a red / blue hat.
What's she wearing?
She's wearing black / pink shoes.

Story

4 Match. Then read and color.

1 My Favorite Hat!

I'm wearing a green hat. It's my favorite hat!

2 What's Tim wearing?

He's wearing a brown hat. It's his favorite hat.

3 What's Maria wearing?

She's wearing a purple hat. It's her favorite hat.

a

b

c

Which clothes are the same? Circle.

THINK BIG

Language in Action

5 **Listen and ✓.**

1 a   b   2 a   b

3 a   b   4 a   b

6 **Look. Read and circle.**

I'm wearing **boots / shoes**, a hat, and a **green / yellow** jacket.

I'm wearing a **green / yellow** T-shirt, pants, and blue **boots / shoes**.

Unit 4 53

Language in Action

7 **Color and write.**

> b = brown g = green o = orange
> p = purple r = red y = yellow

1 He's wearing an orange _____.
2 He's wearing a yellow _____.
3 He's wearing purple _____.
4 He's wearing brown _____.
5 He's wearing green _____.

gloves
hat
pants
shirt
shoes

Social Science | Content Connection

8 Look and ✓.

cold   hot   hot   dry   dry   wet   wet   cold
☐   ☐   ☐   ☐   ☐   ☐   ☐   ☐

9 Find and write. Then listen and circle.

| desert   jungle   mountains |

1

a  It's cold in the _____.
I'm wearing my **hat / T-shirt**.

2

b  It's hot in the _____.
I'm wearing my **shorts / jacket**.

3

c  It's wet in the _____.
I'm wearing my **shoes / boots**.

10 **Look at 9. Read and circle T for true and F for false.**

1 It's hot. I'm wearing my boots.   T   F
2 It's wet. I'm wearing my jacket.   T   F
3 It's cold. I'm wearing my shorts.   T   F
4 It's hot. I'm wearing my hat.   T   F

11 **Look and write. Then color.**

cold   dry   hot   wet

1 _____

2 _____

3 _____

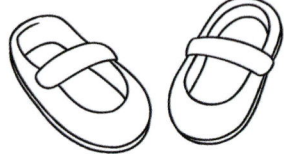
4 _____

It's wet. What's she wearing? Circle.

THINK BIG

dress   jacket   pants   blouse
shorts   shirt   shoes
boots   hat   skirt   socks
gloves

56 Unit 4

Grammar

12 Look at the pictures. Then listen and ✓.

1 She's seven. ☐ 　 2 He's six. ☐ 　 3 They're five. ☐
　 She's nine. ☐ 　　　　 He's ten. ☐ 　　　　 They're eight. ☐

13 Put the words in order. Draw lines.

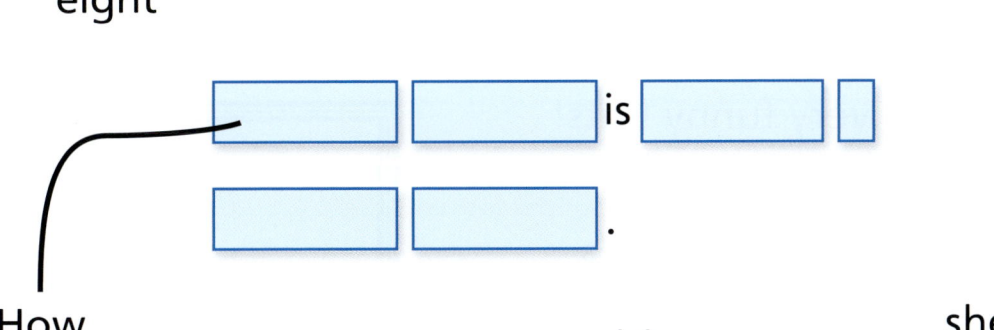

eight　　　　　　　　　　　　　　　　She's

　　　　　　　　　　is

　　　　　　　　　　　　　　　　　　　?

How　　　　　　old　　　　　　　she

14 Read and write.

old　six　ten　two

My name's Mark. I'm six. Ann is my sister. She's young. She's ¹_____. Leo is my brother. He's old. He's ²_____. I have two best friends. They're ³_____, too! Mr. Williams is my teacher. He's very ⁴_____!

Unit 4 57

Culture Connection | Around the World

15 Look and match.

1. I have a black and white hat.
2. I have a pink and purple wool hat.
3. I have a blue cap.

a    b    c

16 Listen and read. Then draw and color.

Here are some very funny hats! Let's look at them.

1. This hat is small. It's a girl's hat. It's yellow. It has a dog on it.

2. This hat is very funny! It's big and blue. It has red pencils on it.

3. This hat is green. It has shoes on it! It has a pink shoe and a purple shoe on it.

17 Look at 16. Read and ✓ or ✗.

1 The small hat is yellow. ☐
2 The big hat has a dog on it. ☐
3 The red pencils are on the blue hat. ☐
4 The shoes are on the green hat. ☐

18 Read and write. Then find and write the word.

1 Some hats have _____ on them.

2 Some hats have many .

3 Some hats have big  on them.

4 Some hats have long _____ on them.

			A			
¹b						
			²c			
		³f				
	⁴f					

People look at the funny hats at A _ _ _ _.

THINK BIG Draw a party hat!

Values | Respect all cultures.

19 Look, read, and write.

dress   pants   white

They're wearing traditional clothes from the Philippines. He's wearing a _____ shirt and _____. She's wearing a white _____.

20 Draw.

I'm wearing traditional clothes.

o, k, ck | Phonics

21 Find and circle the letters **o**, **k**, and **ck**.

22 Read and circle the letters **o**, **k**, and **ck**.

1. on   2. kid   3. sock   4. dog

23 Match the words with the same sounds.

1 pot
2 neck
3 kid

a pick
b kite
c dog

24 Listen and chant.

Put on your socks,
Put on your shorts.
Kick the ball,
Kick, kick, kick!

Review

25 Look and write.

> blouse   boots   dress   gloves   hat   jacket   pants
> shirt   shoes   shorts   skirt   socks   T-shirt

1 _____   2 _____   3 _____   4 _____   5 _____

6 _____   7 _____   8 _____   9 _____

10 _____   11 _____   12 _____   13 _____

62 Unit 4

Review

 26 Look and color. Then listen and ✓.

> 1 = green 2 = yellow 3 = black
> 4 = blue   5 = orange 6 = purple

27 Read, circle, and match.

1 How old **is / are** they?   a I'm eight.
2 How old **is / are** he?   b They're seven.
3 How old **is / are** you?   c She's ten.
4 How old **is / are** she?   d He's three.

Busy at Home

1 Read and match.

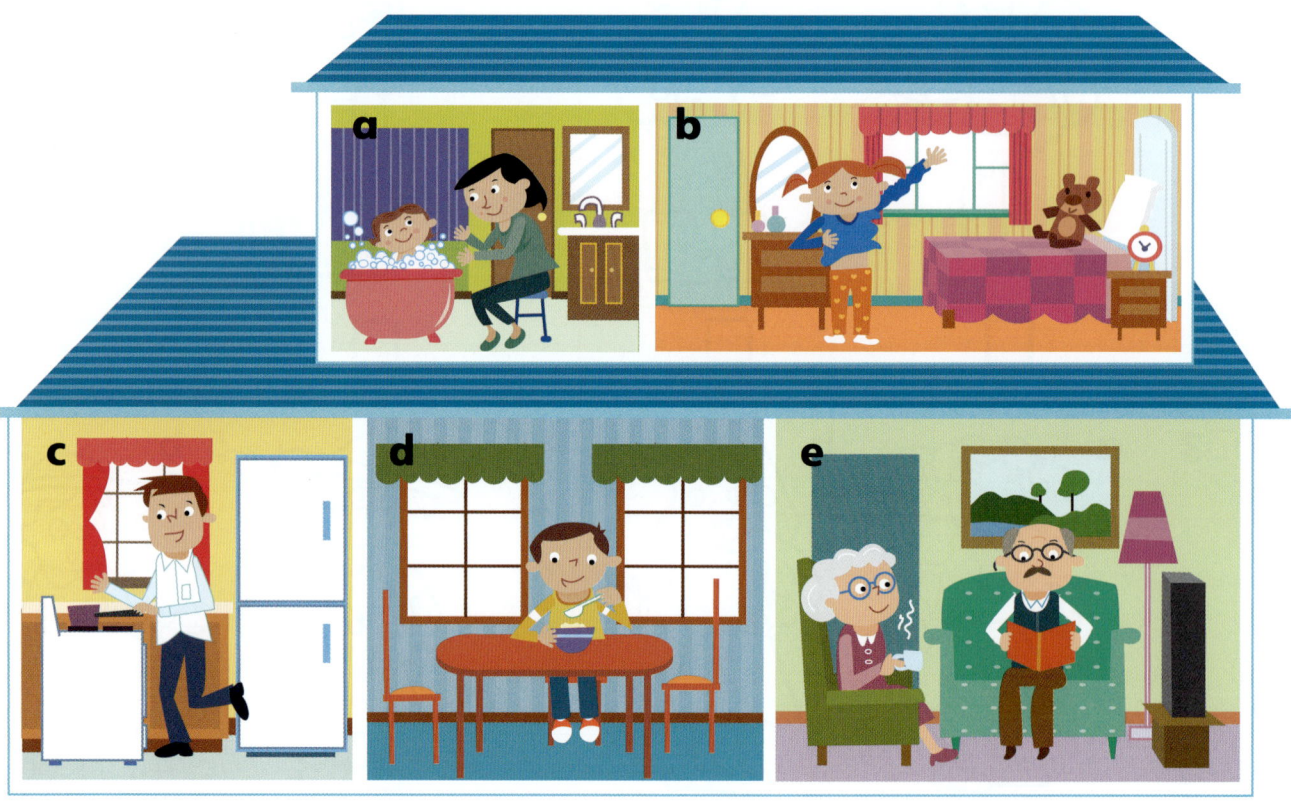

1 She's getting dressed. ☐
2 She's drinking, and he's reading. ☐
3 He's taking a bath. ☐
4 He's making lunch. ☐
5 He's eating. ☐

2. Listen and write. Then sing.

breakfast   face   hair   lunch   phone   teeth

What Are You Doing?

I'm brushing my ¹_____.
I'm combing my ²_____.
   I'm busy. I'm busy.
   What are you doing?

I'm eating my ³_____.
I'm washing my ⁴_____.
   I'm busy. I'm busy.
   What are you doing?

I'm talking on the ⁵_____.
I'm making my ⁶_____.
   I'm busy. I'm busy.
   What are you doing?

Chorus

3. Draw.

He's sleeping.

She's playing.

Story

4 Read and write.

1 What are they doing?
   They're _____.

2 What is Patrick doing?
   He's _____.

3 What's she doing?
   She's _____.

What are you and your friend doing?

We're _____.

Language in Action

 **5** **Listen and number.**

6 **Circle.**

1  **He's / She's** sleeping.

2  **He's / She's** talking on the phone.

3  **He's / She's** drinking.

Unit 5 **67**

Language in Action

7 **Write I'm, He's, or She's.**

1 What's she doing? _____ washing.
2 What are you doing? _____ taking a bath.
3 What's he doing? _____ combing his hair.

8 **Look and match.**

1 What are you doing, Dad?
2 What are you doing, Anna?
3 What are you doing, Mom?
4 What are you doing, Grandpa?

a I'm drawing.
b I'm reading.
c I'm eating.
d I'm making lunch.

9 **Draw. What are you doing?**

I'm _____.

68 Unit 5

Art | **Content Connection**

10 **Read and write.**

apartment   houseboat   lighthouse   yurt

1 _____   2 _____   3 _____   4 _____

11 **Look and listen. Then read and circle.**

1 My home is **a lighthouse** / **an apartment**. It's very tall. It has **six** / **seven** windows. They're **circles** / **squares**. It has one big door. It's a square.

2 This is my home. It's a **yurt** / **houseboat**. It's very small. It has **four** / **five** windows. They're **triangles** / **circles**. The door is a rectangle.

THINK BIG **Find and draw three things in your house that are a square, a circle, and a rectangle.**

Unit 5 **69**

12 Look, read, and ✓ or ✗.

1 It has four small windows. ☐
2 The windows are rectangles. ☐
3 It's an apartment. ☐

4 It has big windows. ☐
5 The table is a triangle. ☐
6 It's a houseboat. ☐

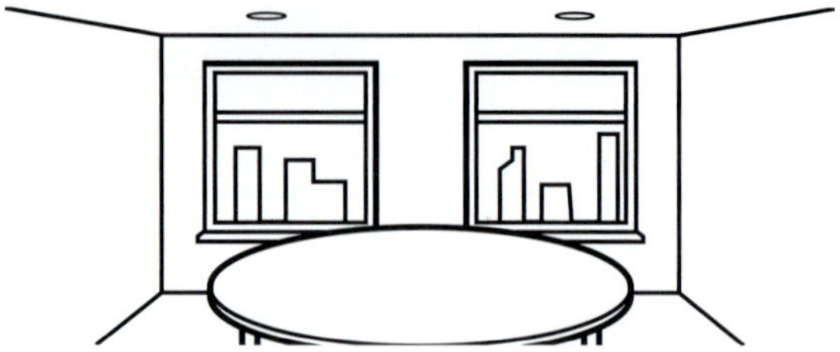

13 Read and draw.

This is my home.
It's a lighthouse.

It's green and white.
It's very tall.

It has six big windows.
They're circles.

It has a square door.
It's brown.

Grammar

 14 Look, read, and match.

1    2    3

a It's small.   b It's orange.   c They're gray.

 15 Put the words in order. Draw lines.

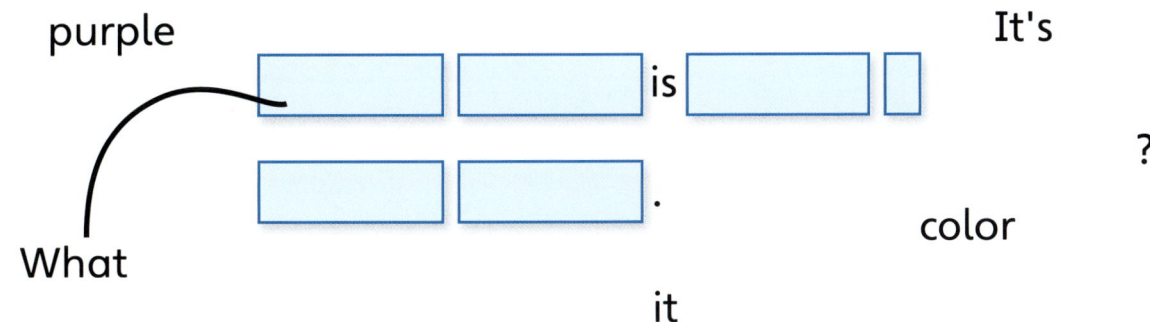

16 Read and circle. Write It's or They're.

1 What color **is** / **are** it?

2 What color is **it** / **they**?

3 What color **is** / **are** they?

_____ orange.   _____ green.   _____ pink.

Unit 5 **71**

Culture Connection | Around the World

17 **Look and circle.**

1 It's **a house / an apartment**.

2 It's **an apartment / a motor home**.

3 It's **a motor home / house**.

18 **Listen, read, and write.**

| big | circle | rectangle | small | square | trailer |

My home is a motor home.
It's in a ¹_____ park.
It has a ²_____ kitchen.
It's a ³_____. It has a living room. The living room has a ⁴_____ TV. It's a ⁵_____. I have a small bedroom. It has a window. It's a ⁶_____. My home is comfortable.

19 **Look at 18. Circle T for true and F for false.**

1 My home is an apartment. T F
2 It has a big kitchen. T F
3 The living room is a rectangle. T F
4 The bedroom is small. T F
5 The bedroom window is a circle. T F

20 **Read and match.**

1 There are eight chairs in the   a bedroom.
2 Mom and Dad sleep in the   b kitchen.
3 The big TV is in the   c dining room.
4 There's a very small table in the d living room.

THINK BIG Draw a living room. How many shapes can you use?

Unit 5 73

Values | Help at home.

21 Listen and write.

cleaning   drying   helping   washing

1 She's _____ her room.

2 She's _____ the dishes.

3 He's _____ the dishes.

4 She's _____ her mom.

22 Draw.

I'm helping at home.

u, f, ff | **Phonics**

23 Find and circle the letters **u**, **f**, and **ff**.

24 Read and circle the letters **u**, **f**, and **ff**.

1. up 2. fan 3. puff 4. bus

25 Match the words with the same sounds.

1. sun   **a** fan
2. off   **b** up
3. fog   **c** puff

26 Listen and chant.

We're having fun,
Running in the sun.
Up, up, up!
Puff, puff, puff!

Unit 5 **75**

Review

27 Look, read, and match.

a 　　b

1　I'm brushing my teeth.

2　I'm taking a bath.

c 　　d

3　I'm making lunch.

4　I'm eating.

e 　　f

5　I'm sleeping.

6　I'm playing.

7　I'm combing my hair.

g 　　h

8　I'm drinking.

9　I'm reading.

10　I'm talking on the phone.

i 　　j

11　I'm washing my face.

12　I'm getting dressed.

k 　　l

Review

28 **Look and write.**

> are   is   It's   they   They're   What

1

Look at the book.

What color _____ it?

_____ blue.

2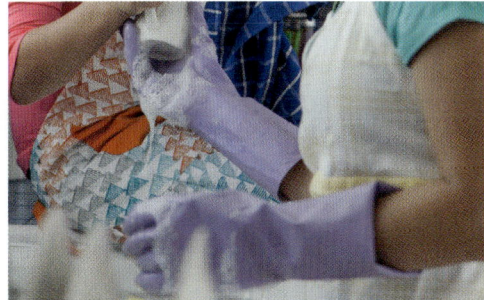

Look at the gloves.

_____ color _____ _____?

_____ purple.

29 **Color the shapes. What is it?**

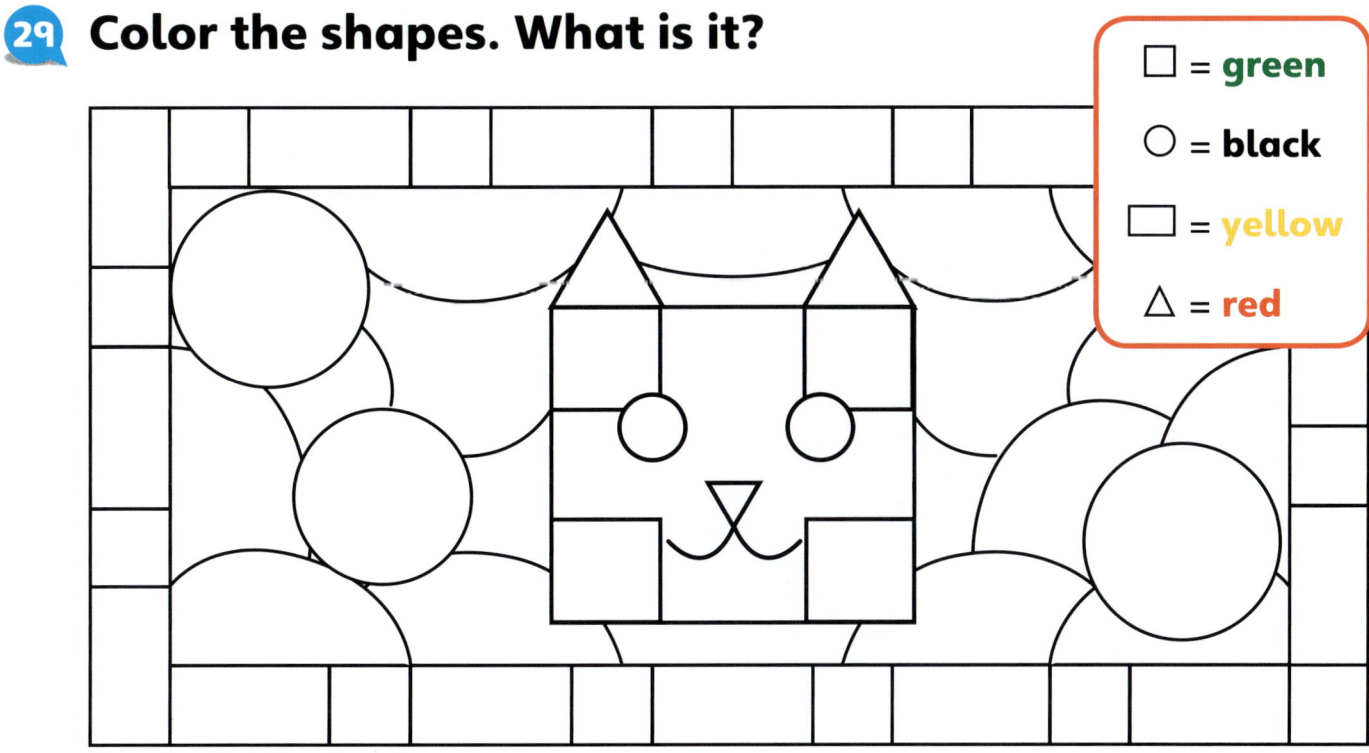

□ = green
○ = black
▭ = yellow
△ = red

What is it?   It's a c__t.

Unit 5 77

unit 6
On the Farm

1 Look and write. Then circle.

cow   duck   horse

1

It's a _____.
It's **eating** / **flying**.

2

It's a _____.
It's **sleeping** / **running**.

3

It's a _____.
It's **running** / **flying**.

2. Listen and match. Then chant.

Look at the Animals

Look over here!
Look over there!
There are animals
Everywhere!

What is it?
It's a **duck**.
What's it doing?
It's flying up high!

What is it?
It's a **dog**!
What's it doing?
It's jumping with the **frogs**!

What are they?
They're **goats**!
What are they doing?
They're eating some oats!

Chorus

a
b
c
d

3. Write. Then draw.

This is my favorite farm animal. Look. It's a _____.

Story

4 Read and number.

Oh, no! It's eating your skirt! ☐   It's jumping. ☐   They're running. ☐   It's flying. ☐

THINK BIG Which sentence is wrong? Check (✓) or cross (✗).
The frog is jumping. ☐   The cat is flying. ☐
The horse is running. ☐

Language in Action

5 Listen and number.

6 Look and write.

eating   flying   jumping   running

1 It's _____.

2 It's _____.

3 It's _____.

4 It's _____.

Language in Action

7 **Look and circle.**

1 It's / **They're** jumping.   2 **It's** / They're eating.

3 **It's** / They're flying.   4 It's / **They're** running.

8 **Draw.**

What's the cat doing?
It's sleeping.

Social Science | Content Connection

 Listen. Then color, match, and circle.

| 1 This cow is … | 2 This chicken is … | 3 This dog is … | 4 This cat is … |

a
A baby chicken is called a **calf** / **chick**.

b
A baby dog is called a **kitten** / **puppy**.

c
A baby cat is called a **calf** / **kitten**.

d
A baby cow is called a **puppy** / **calf**.

THINK BIG

Circle the picture that is wrong.

a  b  c

10 Look and write.

cat   chick   chicken   dog   kitten   puppy

1. A baby _____ is called a _____.

2. A baby _____ is called a _____.

3. A baby _____ is called a _____.

11 What's your favorite baby animal? Draw and write.

My favorite baby animal is a _____.

A _____ is a baby _____.

Grammar

12 **Look, listen, and number.**

a

b

c

d

e

f

13 **Complete the chart.**

| he | her | I | its | their | your |

1 _____	my
you	2 _____
3 _____	his
she	4 _____
it	5 _____
we	our
they	6 _____

Unit 6   85

Culture Connection | Around the World

14 Look and circle.

1 horse / snake   2 rabbit / hamster   3 mouse / dog   4 cat / canary

15 Listen, read, and match.

1 I have a pet canary. He's yellow. His name's Tom Bird.

2 This is my pet snake. She's green. Her name's Samantha.

3 I have a pet mouse. She's small and white. Her name's Zoe.

4 I have a pet hamster. He's brown. His name's Charlie.

a

b

c

d

16 Look at 15. Read and write.

brown   green   white   yellow

1 The pet hamster is _____.
2 The pet canary is _____.
3 The pet mouse is _____.
4 The pet snake is _____.

17 Find and write the words.

1 _____   ncayra
2 _____   mharets
3 _____   uesmo
4 _____   eknsa

Draw a bad pet!

THINK BIG

Unit 6 87

Values | Be nice to animals.

18 Listen and write. Then match.

brushing   feeding   playing   walking

a

b

c

d

1 I'm _____ the dog.

2 I'm _____ with the cat.

3 I'm _____ the chickens.

4 I'm _____ the horse.

19 Draw.

I'm playing with the cat.

r, h, j | Phonics

20 Find and circle the letters r, h, and j.

21 Read and circle the letters r, h, and j.

1 rat   2 hat   3 jam   4 run

22 Match the words with the same sounds.

1 red   a hut
2 hen   b rock
3 jam   c job

23 Listen and chant.

A red hen in
A red hat
Is eating red jam.
Run, red hen, run!

Review

24 **Look, read, and circle.**

1

1 It's a **dog** / **cat**.

2 It's a **goat** / **dog**.

2

3

3 It's a **cow** / **sheep**.

4 It's a **frog** / **sheep**.

4

5 It's a **turtle** / **horse**.

5

6 It's a **chicken** / **horse**.

7 It's a **duck** / **chicken**.

6

7

8 It's a **frog** / **dog**.

9 It's a **cat** / **chicken**.

8

9

10 It's a **goat** / **cow**.

10

Review

25 **Look and read. Then circle and write.**

| eating | flying | jumping | running | sleeping |

What are they doing?

1 What are they doing?
 It's / They're
 _____.

2 What's it doing?
 It's / They're
 _____.

3 What are they doing?
 It's / They're
 _____.

4 What's it doing?
 It's / They're
 _____.

5 What are they doing?
 It's / They're
 _____.

26 **Read and write.**

| Her | His | Its | my | our | your |

I have a hamster and a cat. They're ¹_____ pets. My brother has a snake. ²_____ snake is green and brown.

My sister has a canary. ³_____ canary is very small. ⁴_____ feathers are yellow. There are four pets in ⁵_____ family!

Do you have a pet in ⁶_____ house?

Unit 6 91

Checkpoint | Units 4–6

1 Look, find, and number.

2 Look and ✓.
What is Sue wearing?

- ☐ a hat
- ☐ a T-shirt
- ☐ boots
- ☐ pants
- ☐ a jacket

🔍 **CLOTHES**

1 dress
2 shoes
3 pants
4 shirt

Look at **1** and draw.
What other animals can you see?

Unit 7 Party Time

1 Match.

1

2

milk | fruit
a | b
c | d
juice | pizza

3

4

2 Look at 1. Write.

1 She's drinking _____. 2 He's drinking _____.

3 They're eating _____. 4 She's eating _____.

3 Listen and number. Then sing.

a

b

It's My Party!

Welcome, friends.
Please sit down.
It's time for my party!
With games and a clown!

I have pizza, **chicken**, (1)
Salad, too. (2)
Fruit, **cake** (3)
And **ice cream** for you! (4)

Or put some **pasta** (5)
On your plate.
With juice or **milk** (6)
It sure tastes great.

Thanks for the presents.
What a great day!
Let's eat and drink
And play, play, play.

d

c

f

e

4 Draw.

I'm eating fries and I'm drinking water.

Unit 7 **95**

Story

5 Read and write.

1 Tim's party is on _____.

2 Tim has _____.

3 Maria has _____.

4 Patrick has _____ and _____.

Write the days in order. Then circle your favorite day.

_____ Monday _____ _____

Thursday _____ Saturday

Language in Action

6 **Look and write.**

> I have fruit.   I have pizza.

What do you have?

1 _____

2 _____

7 **Read and draw.**

1 I have chicken.

2 I have ice cream.

Unit 7 **97**

Language in Action

8 Draw. Then write.

cake   fruit   ice cream   juice   pizza

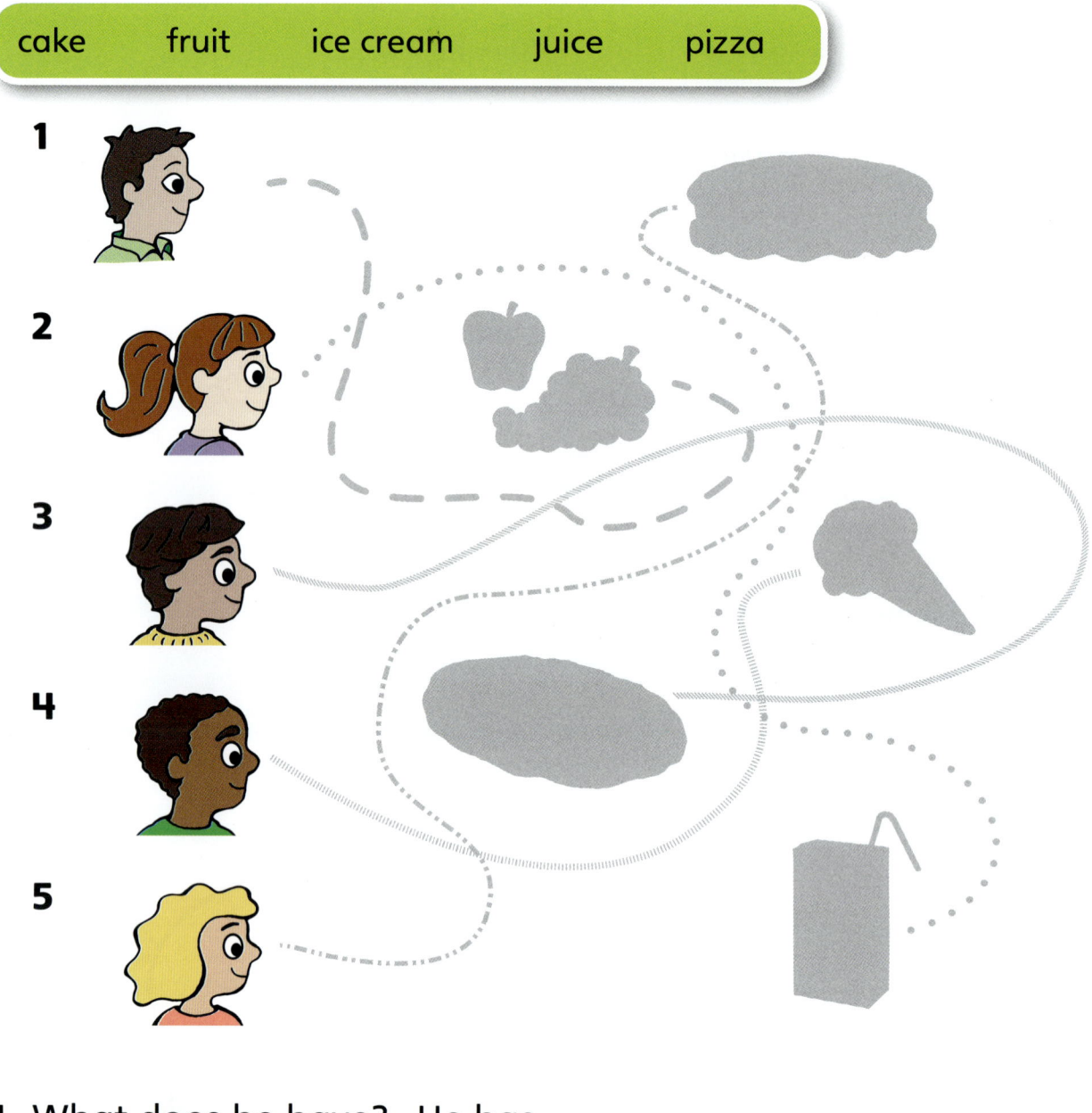

1 What does he have? He has _____.
2 What does she have? She has _____.
3 What does he have? He _____.
4 What does he have? _____
5 What does she have? _____

Science | Content Connection

9 Look and write.

chips   chocolate   cookies   fries   salt   sugar

1. _____
2. _____
3. _____
4. _____
5. _____
6. _____

10 Listen, read, and circle.

Some foods are salty, and some are sweet. Chocolate is my favorite ¹**salty** / **sweet** food, and pizza is my favorite ²**salty** / **sweet** food.

Fries are ³**salty** / **sweet**, and chips are ⁴**salty** / **sweet**, too. They have ⁵**salt** / **sugar** on them.

Cookies, cake, and ice cream are all ⁶**salty** / **sweet**. They have ⁷**salt** / **sugar** in them.

Draw and write.

THINK BIG

_____ sweet.

_____ salty.

11 **Look and write sweet or salty.**

1. are _____.
2. is _____.
3. are _____.
4. is _____.
5. is _____.
6. are _____.

12 **Find and circle.**

cake   chips   chocolate   cookies
fries   ice cream   salty   sweet

p	i	t	e	k	o	c	h	i	p	s
c	h	o	c	o	l	a	t	e	o	a
h	b	i	c	p	o	k	a	w	s	l
o	i	c	e	c	r	e	a	m	w	t
b	i	s	c	o	o	k	i	e	s	y
f	r	d	n	c	d	f	r	i	e	s
r	e	n	f	r	s	w	e	e	t	y

100   Unit 7

Grammar

13 Look, read, and .

1

a He doesn't drink juice. ☐
b He don't drink juice. ☐

2

a She don't eat cake. ☐
b She doesn't eat cake. ☐

3

a They doesn't ride their bikes. ☐
b They don't ride their bikes. ☐

4

a We don't play soccer. ☐
b We doesn't play soccer. ☐

14 Write **don't** or **doesn't** and match.

1 I _____ eat   a to work.
2 She _____ go   b TV.
3 It _____ drink   c pasta.
4 They _____ watch   d milk.

Unit 7 **101**

Culture Connection | Around the World

15 Look and circle.

1 candy / cake   2 ice cream / soup   3 pizza / pie

**16 Listen, read, and match.**

   1 I'm Minjoon. It's my birthday! I have seaweed soup. It's salty! I'm from…   **a** Russia.

   2 My name's Lily. I have a big cake on my birthday. It's very sweet! I'm from…   **b** Mexico.

   3 I'm Dimitri. On my birthday I have fruit pie. It has sugar in it. Mmm! I'm from…   **c** South Korea.

   4 My name's Anita. I have candy in a piñata on my birthday. Piñatas are from…   **d** the United States of America.

17 Look at **16**. Complete the chart.

1 _____	the United States	cake
Minjoon	South Korea	2 _____
3 _____	Russia	pie
Anita	4 _____	candy

18 Read and find. Write the words.

ACROSS

3 a sweet food

5 a favorite day

DOWN

1 ____ are from Mexico.

2 ____ in a pinata

4 a fruit ____

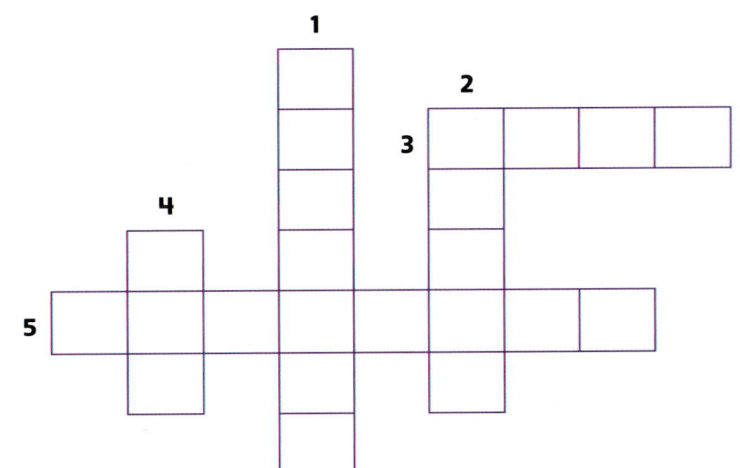

THINK BIG

What do people have on their birthday in your country? Draw.

Unit 7 103

Values | Eat three meals a day.

19 Look and write.

breakfast   dinner   lunch

1 I eat _____ every day.

2 I eat _____ every day.

3 I eat _____ every day.

20 Draw.

This is my dinner. I'm eating _____ and _____. I'm drinking _____.

104 Unit 7

l, ll, v, w | **Phonics**

21 Find and circle the letters **l**, **ll**, **v**, and **w**.

22 Read and circle the letters **l**, **ll**, **v**, and **w**.

1  2  3  4

23 Match the words with the same sounds.

1 let   a sell
2 bell   b leg
3 vet   c win
4 we   d van

24 Listen and chant.

Let's ring the bell
For the vet
With the van!

Review

25 Listen and match. Then write.

1 I have _____.
2 I have _____.
3 I have _____.
4 I have _____.
5 I have _____.

water   salad   chicken   pasta   fries

26 Look and write.

1 What does he have?

_____

_____

2 What does she have?

_____

_____

106 Unit 7

Review

27 **Write I have, He has, or She has.**

1 What do you have?
_____
milk.

2 What does he have?
_____
pizza.

3 What does she have?
_____
juice.

28 **Color. Then match and read.**

1 I have    a fruit.

2 Mom has    b cake.

3 Dad has    c ice cream.

29 **Read and circle.**

1 We **don't** / **doesn't** have a pet.

2 Sally **do** / **doesn't** have soup on her birthday.

3 You **don't** / **doesn't** sing in the class.

4 The dog **do** / **doesn't** eat candy.

Fun and Games

1 Listen and number.

2 Look at **1** and write.

action figure   ball   blocks   car   puppet   train

1 This is my _____.
2 This is my _____.
3 These are my _____.
4 This is my _____.
5 This is my _____.
6 This is my _____.

108 Unit 8

3 Listen and circle. Then sing.

What's In Your Toy Box?

Kim, what's in your toy box?
Do you have a plane / bike?
No, but this is my blue car / game.
And where's my gray train?

Kim, what's on your toy shelf?
Do you have a ball / doll?
Yes, yes, here it is.
And here's my purple doll / car.

Kim, what's on your table?
Do you have big blocks / stuffed animals?
Yes, and these are my puppets / trains.
My favorite's Mr. Fox!

These are my favorite toys,
Purple, green, and gray.
I share my toys with my friends
And I play every day!

4 Draw toys.

Story

5 Read and write.

1 Where's the doll?
_____

2 Where are the action figures?
_____

Look. Circle three differences.

Language in Action

6 **Read and number.**

1 It's under the desk.

2 They're on the shelf.

3 It's in the toy box.

a

c

b

7 **Write in, on, or under.**

1 _____

2 _____

3 _____

4 _____

5 _____

6 _____

8 **Circle the words and write.**

1 x x x i n x x x x x x   _____
2 x x x x x u n d e r x x   _____
3 x x i n x x x x o n x x   _____ _____

Unit 8   111

Language in Action

9 Trace and draw.

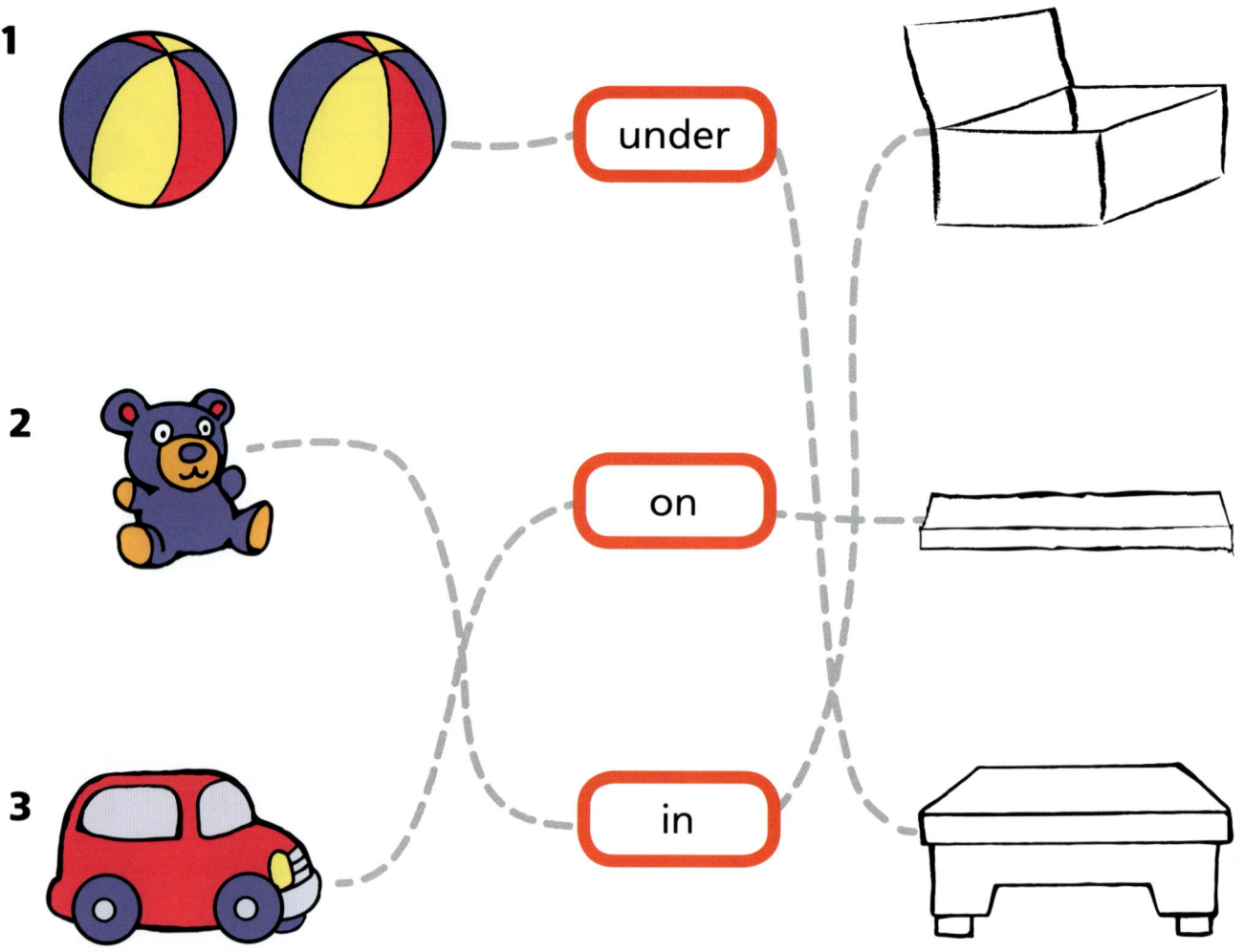

10 Look at **9** and circle.

1 Where are the balls?
The balls are **in** / **on** / **under** the table.

2 Where is the stuffed animal?
The stuffed animal is **in** / **on** / **under** the toy box.

3 Where is the car?
The car is **in** / **on** / **under** the shelf.

Art | **Content Connection**

11 **Look and match.**

1 2 3 4 5
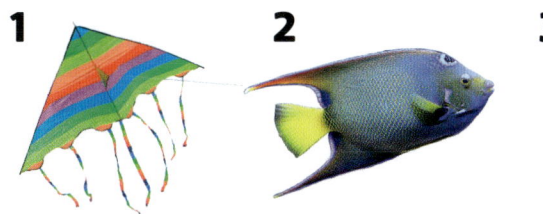  

a dragon   **b** butterfly   **c** kite   **d** fish   **e** bird

12 **Listen and read. Then match and color.**

a   b   c   d
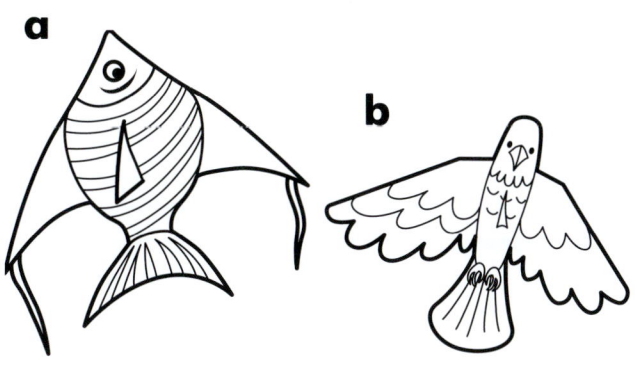 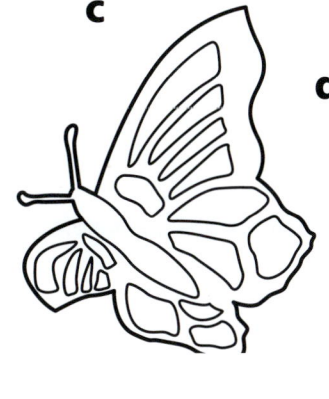 

1 This kite looks like a butterfly. It's flying high in the sky. It's big and purple.

2 This kite looks like a bird. It's yellow and brown. This is my favorite kite.

3 This kite looks like a dragon. It's long and very colorful. It's red, orange, and green.

4 This is my kite. It looks like a fish. It's blue and red.

13 Look at **12**. Read and circle **T** for true and **F** for false.

1 The purple kite looks like a dragon. T F
2 The blue and red kite looks like a fish. T F
3 The colorful kite looks like a butterfly. T F
4 The yellow and brown kite looks like a bird. T F

14 Find and write the words.

1 _____ rgnoda
2 _____ drib
3 _____ yflubrett
4 _____ hifs

Guess. Then connect the dots and write.

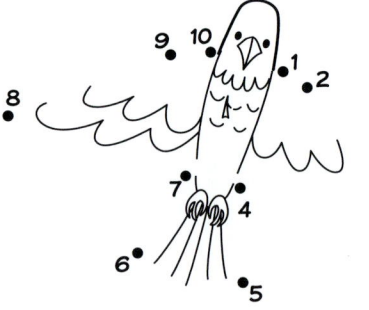

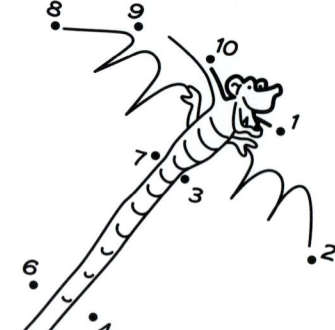

1 This kite looks like a _____.

2 This kite looks like a _____.

114 Unit 8

Grammar

15 Look and write There is or There are.

1 _____ a game.　　2 _____ four cars.

 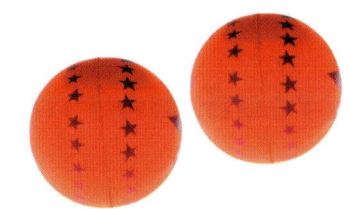

3 _____ a puppet.　　4 _____ two balls.

16 Look at 15. Read and circle.

1 Is there a game?　　　　　　　Yes, there is. / No, there isn't.
2 Are there five cars?　　　　　　Yes, there are. / No, there aren't.
3 Is there a stuffed animal?　　　Yes, there is. / No, there isn't.
4 Are there two balls?　　　　　　Yes, there are. / No, there aren't.

17 Read and write Is there or Are there.

1 _____ an action figure on the shelf?
2 _____ twelve kites in the sky?
3 _____ dolls in the toy box?
4 _____ a sandwich on the table?

Culture Connection | Around the World

18 Look and circle.

1 This train is **wool / wooden**.

2 These are **Russian / wool** dolls.

3 These cars are **colorful / wooden**.

19 Listen, read, and match.

1
This is my toy box. It has my toys in it. Let's look at them.

a

2
This is my favorite doll. It's from the U.K. It's a girl. She's wearing a wool hat and a pink dress.

b

3
These blocks are very old. They're Dad's blocks. They're wooden. They're from Australia. There are red, blue, green, and yellow blocks.

c

116 Unit 8

20 Look at 19. Read and match.

1 There are toys　　　　　　　　a her favorite.
2 The doll is　　　　　　　　　　b very old.
3 The blocks come from　　　　 c in the toy box.
4 They're　　　　　　　　　　　d Australia.

21 Read and write.

| colorful　favorite　Russian　wooden　wool |

1 My _____ toy is my kite.
2 This stuffed animal is wearing a _____ jacket.
3 His bike is red, blue, and green. It's very _____.
4 Her action figure is old. It's _____.
5 These dolls are not from the U.K. They're _____.

THINK BIG

What's your favorite toy? Draw and write.

My favorite toy is _____.

Unit 8 117

Values | Share your toys.

22 **Match.**

a   b    c

1. OK. Thank you!
2. Sharing is fun!
3. Here's my car. Let's share.

23 **Draw.**

I share my toys with _____.

qu, x, y | Phonics

24 Find and circle the letters qu, x, and y.

25 Read and circle the letters qu, x, and y.

1 six   2 quick   3 yell   4 box

26 Match the words with the same sounds.

1 quick   a yes
2 fox   b box
3 yum   c quack

27 Listen and chant.

Six quick foxes,
In a yellow box!

Review

28 Look and match. Then read.

John's toys

1
2
3
4
5

Jane's toys

6
7
8
9
10

a action figure

b ball

c blocks

d plane

e bike

f stuffed animal

g train

h doll

i puppet

j game

29 Read and draw.

Where are the cars?
They're in the toy box.

Where's the ball?
It's on the cars.

Review

30 Listen and number.

31 Read and circle. Then look at **30** and ✓ or ✗.

1 **There is** / **There are** a plane on the shelf.
2 **There is** / **There are** three action figures under the chair.
3 **There is** / **There are** a blue ball in the toy box.
4 **There is** / **There are** two stuffed animals on the chair.

32 Look at **30**. Count and write.

How many toys can you see? _____

Unit 9 — Play Time

1 Follow the path. Write.

> catching   dancing   hitting   jumping rope   kicking
> riding   running   singing   skating   throwing

1 _____
2 _____
3 _____
4 _____
5 _____
6 _____
7 _____
8 _____
9 _____
10 _____

2 Listen and sing. Then match.

Play Time Is Cool!

We like play time at our school.
Singing and dancing,
Throwing and catching.
Play time is cool at our school!

I'm throwing the ball.
It's so much fun!
Are you hitting and running?
Yes, and it's fun.

We're kicking the ball
And trying to score.
It's so much fun.
Let's play some more.

Chorus

3 Look at 2 and write.

1 She is _____ the ball.
2 He is _____ the ball.
3 He is _____ .
4 She is _____ the ball.

4 What are you doing? Draw and write.

I'm _____
_____

Unit 9 123

Story

5 **Read. Then write.**

1 What's Patrick doing in picture 1?

He's _____.

2 What are the boys doing in picture 2?

They're _____.

3 What are the boys doing in picture 3?

They're _____.

THINK BIG

What do you do before bed?

Look at me. I'm _____.

Language in Action

6 Look and ✓.

Is Tom skating?

☐ Yes, he is.
☐ No, he isn't.

Is Jen jumping rope?

☐ Yes, she is.
☐ No, she isn't.

7 Look and write the answer.

Yes, they are.
No, they aren't.

1

Are they playing?

_____

2

Are they jumping?

_____

Language in Action

8 **Look, listen, and circle.**

1

Yes, he is. /
No, he isn't.

2

Yes, she is. /
No, she isn't.

3

Yes, they are. /
No, they aren't.

4

Yes, they are. /
No, they aren't.

9 **Look and write.**

1

Are they playing?
Yes, _____.

2

Are they kicking a ball?
No, _____.
They're jumping rope.

Physical Education | Content Connection

10 Look and match.

1 hide and seek

2 climbing

3 tag

4 jumping rope

5 hopscotch

a

b

c

d

e

11 Listen, read, and write.

| climbing | hide and seek | hopscotch | jump rope | tag |

1 Katie and Simon are playing _____. I'm playing, too. It's our favorite game. Hop! Hop! Hop!

2 Emily is _____ the tree. Up! Up! She's at the top! It's very high.

3 The boys are playing _____ on the school playground. George is looking for his friends. Where are they?

4 Tom and Dan are playing _____ with my brother. Run, Dan! Run! Tag, you're it, Tom!

5 My sisters _____ on the playground. It's a lot of fun. Jump! Jump! Jump!

12 **Look at 11. Read and ✓ or ✗.**

1 Simon's favorite game is hopscotch. ☐
2 Emily is jumping rope on the playground. ☐
3 George is at the top of the tree. ☐
4 My brother is playing tag. ☐
5 My sisters are playing hide and seek. ☐

13 **Find and write the words.**

b i m l c n g i   n g i u p m j o p e r

1 _____   2 _____

e h i d n d a e k e s   p h o c h t o s c   a g t

3 _____   4 _____   5 _____

What games do you play? Write.

I _____.

Grammar

14 **Look and circle.**

1 I **like** / **don't like** fruit.

2 She **likes** / **doesn't like** dancing.

3 He **likes** / **doesn't like** frogs.

4 I **like** / **don't like** salad.

15 **Read and write.**

| doesn't | don't | like | likes |

1 She _____ like snakes.

2 I don't _____ playing tag.

3 He _____ apples.

4 I _____ like singing.

16 **Draw and write.**

1 I like _____.

2 I don't like _____.

Culture Connection | Around the World

17 Look and circle.

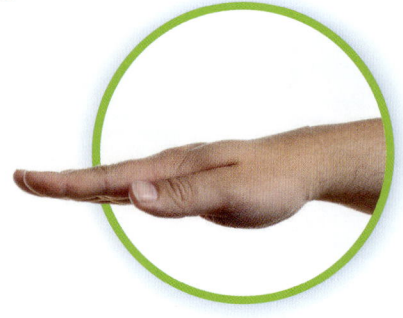  

1 paper / rock   2 scissors / rock   3 paper / scissors

18 Listen, read, and match.

1 I'm _____. I'm eight, and I'm from Chile. I play a game called Cachipún. My brother is the best player.

a
Michio

2 I'm _____, and I'm nine. I'm from Canada. I play Rock, Paper, Scissors with my sisters and my best friend. I always win.

b
Raúl

3 I'm _____ from Japan. I'm seven. I play this game called Janken at lunch with my friends. I sometimes win.

c
Eva

130 Unit 9

19 Look at 18. Read and write the country.

Canada   Chile   Japan

1 Janken   _____

2 Rock, Paper, Scissors   _____

3 Cachipún   _____

20 Read and draw.

1 Paper covers rock. Paper wins!

2 Scissors cut paper. Scissors win!

3 Rock breaks scissors. Rock wins!

THINK BIG What other game do you play with your hands? Draw.

Values | Take care of your body.

21 Match and write.

drink   enough   food   sleep

1

a Get enough _____ and _____.

2

b Get _____ exercise.

3

c Get enough _____.

22 Draw.

I take care of my body.

ss, z, zz | **Phonics**

23 Find and circle the letters **ss**, **z**, and **zz**.

24 Read and circle the letters **ss**, **z**, and **zz**.

1 fizz   2 mess   3 zap   4 miss

25 Match the words with the same sounds.

1 zip   a zap
2 buzz   b hiss
3 miss   c fizz

26 Listen and chant.

Buzz goes the bee.
Zip, zap!
It misses me!

Unit 9 **133**

Review

27 Look, read, and number.

1 He's catching a ball.
2 He's throwing a ball.
3 She's kicking a ball.
4 He's jumping rope.
5 He likes singing.
6 She likes dancing.

28 Draw an activity. Then write.

I'm _____.

Review

29 Listen and number.

30 Read and ✓ or ✗ for you.

1 I get enough exercise.

2 I like hide and seek.

3 I play hopscotch.

4 I get enough sleep.

5 I get enough food and drink.

6 I like tag.

Checkpoint | Units 7–9

1. **Look, find, and number.**

2. **Look and ✓.**
   What does he have?

My Party List
- ☐ cars
- ☐ a bike
- ☐ a game
- ☐ a puppet
- ☐ a train

TOYS

1 action figure
2 bike
3 game
4 puppet

3. **Think and draw.**
   What is in the present?

🔍 PARTY FOOD

5 cake
6 fruit
7 juice

🔍 PLAY TIME

8 catching
9 kicking
10 throwing

Unit 1 | Extra Grammar Practice

> What **is** it?   It**'s** a chair.

1 **Write and color.**

1 What is it? 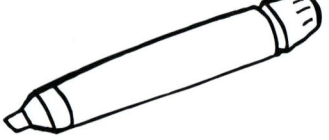 ____ a marker. It's blue.

2 What _____ it? 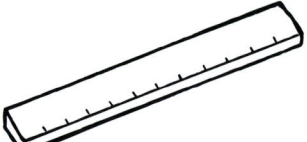 ____ a ruler. It's yellow.

3 _____ is it?  ____ a backpack. It's red.

4 What is _____ ?  ____ a crayon. It's green.

5 _____ _____ it? 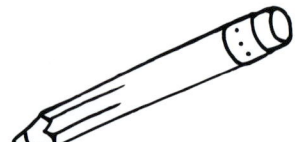 ____ a pencil. It's blue.

6 What _____ _____ ?  ____ a book. It's red.

2 **Connect numbers 1 to 10. Look and circle.**

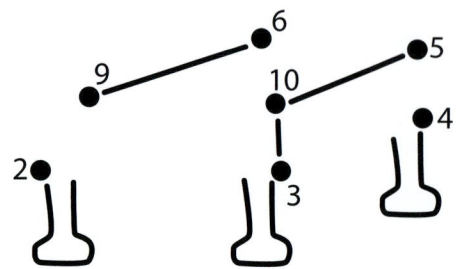

What is it?

It's a **chair** / **desk**.

138 Unit 1

Extra Grammar Practice | Unit 2

How many brothers and sisters **do** you **have**?
I have one brother.
I have two sisters.

1 **Write and match.**

1. I _____ three sisters.
2. I _____ two brothers.
3. I _____ one brother and one sister.
4. I _____ one sister.
5. I _____ two sisters and one brother.

a. 
b. 
c. 
d. 
e.

2 **Draw a monster family.**

3 **Look at 2. Count and write.**

How many monsters? _____

Unit 3 | Extra Grammar Practice

Does she have long hair?	Yes, she does.
Does he have short hair?	No, he doesn't.
Does it have a small head?	Yes, it does.
Does it have a big head?	No, it doesn't.

1 Look and match.

1 Does she have a long nose?

2 Does she have short hair?

3 Does she have long arms?

4 Does she have big feet?

5 Does he have a long nose?

6 Does he have short hair?

7 Does he have long arms?

8 Does he have big feet?

Yes, she does.

No, she doesn't.

Yes, he does.

No, he doesn't.

2 Look at the dog. Write.

1 It has long _____.

2 It has a big _____.

Extra Grammar Practice | Unit 4

> What **are** you **wearing**?   I**'m wearing** a green hat.
>
> What**'s** he/she **wearing**?   He**'s**/She**'s wearing** white pants.

1 **What's she wearing? Write and color.**

1 _____ a red blouse.

2 _____ a yellow skirt.

3 _____ brown shoes.

2 **Read and color.**

What are you wearing?

I'm wearing a red jacket and brown pants.

I'm wearing an orange dress and purple shoes.

Unit 5 | Extra Grammar Practice

> What **are** you **doing**?   **I'm** reading.
> What**'s** she **doing**?   **She's** making lunch.

1 Look and write.

1 What are you doing, Jim?

_____ water.

2 What are you doing, Ellen?

_____ a book.

3 What are you doing, Ben?

_____ my teeth.

4 What are you doing, Pam?

_____ to my dad.

2 Look at 1. Write.

1 What's Jim doing? He's _____.

2 What's Ellen doing? _____ reading.

3 What's Ben _____? _____

4 What's Dad _____? _____ watching TV.

142 Unit 5

Extra Grammar Practice | Unit 6

What's the duck doing?	It's swimming.
What are the cows doing?	They're eating.
What's he/she doing?	He's/She's running.

1 Look and match. What are they doing?

1

a sleeping

2

b running

3

c swimming

4

d eating

2 Read. Circle and write.

1 What's he doing?    He's / They're _____.

2 What are the cats doing?    She's / They're _____.

3 What's she doing?    She's / He's _____.

4 What's it doing?    It's / They're _____.

Unit 7 | Extra Grammar Practice

> What **does** he **have**?   He **has** milk.
> What **do** you **have**?   I **have** juice.

1 Look and write.

1 What does he have?   He has **cake** / **milk**.

2 What does she have? She has **fruit** / **pasta**.

3 What do you have?   I have **pizza** / **chocolate**.

4 What do they have?   They have **chips** / **juice**.

2 Write has or have. Then match.

1 I _____ juice.   a

2 She _____ chicken.   b

3 They _____ fries.   c

4 He _____ ice cream.   d

Extra Grammar Practice | Unit 8

Where's the ball?	It's **in** the toy box. It's **on** the shelf. It's **under** the table.
Where are the cars?	They're **under** the desk. They're **on** the couch.

1 Write **Where's** or **Where are**. Then match.

1 _____ the action figures?

2 _____ the car?

3 _____ the blocks?

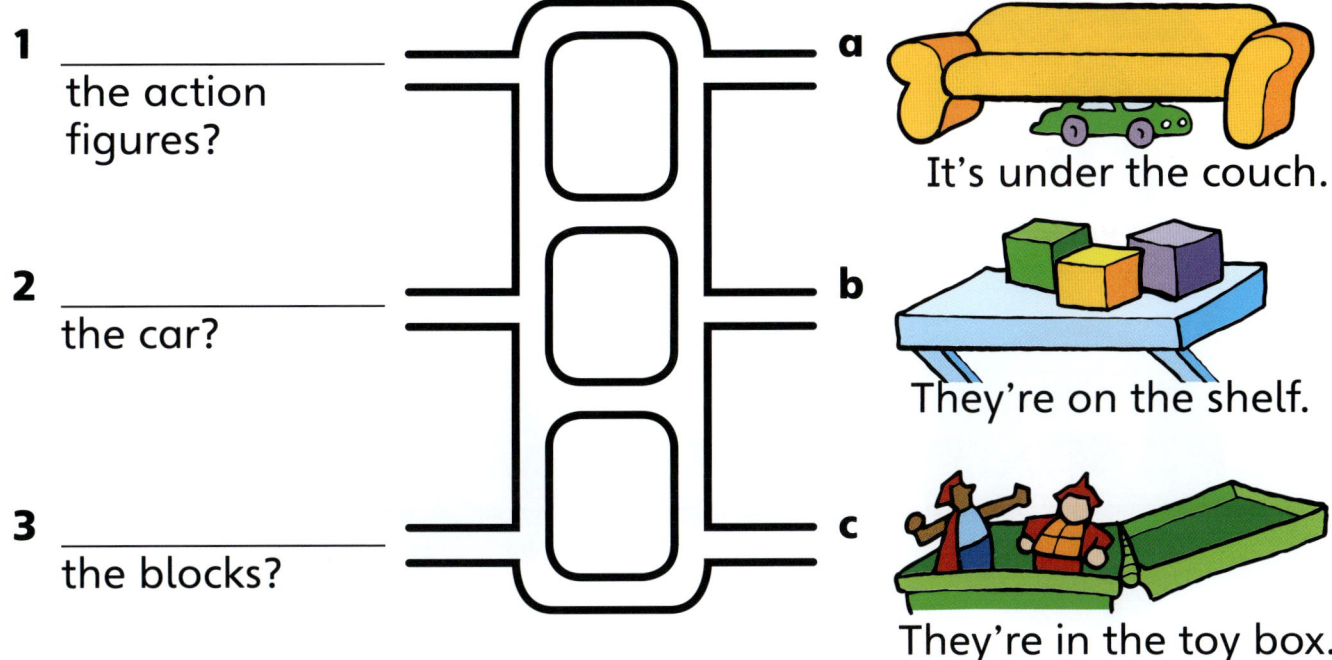

a It's under the couch.

b They're on the shelf.

c They're in the toy box.

2 Look and write **in**, **on**, or **under**.

1 Where's the ball?

It's _____ the desk.

2 Where are the balls?

They're _____ the desk.

3 Where's the ball?

It's _____ the desk.

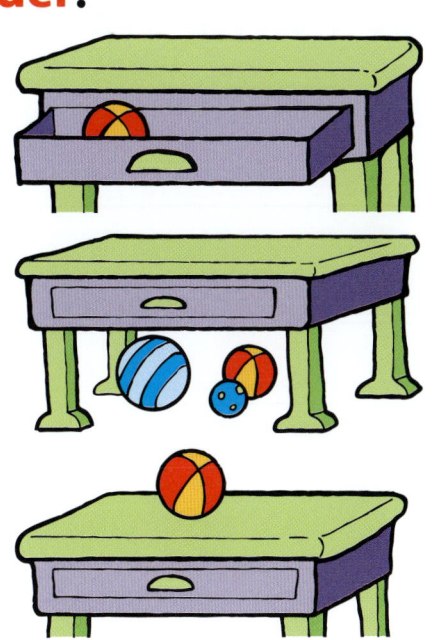

Unit 8 **145**

Unit 9 | Extra Grammar Practice

| **Is** she **singing**? | Yes, she **is**. | No, she **isn't**. |
| **Are** they **dancing**? | Yes, they **are**. | No, they **aren't**. |

1 Read. Look and write.

1  Is she throwing the ball?

Yes, she _____.

2  Is he running?

No, he _____.

3  Are they sleeping?

No, they _____.

4  Are they jumping rope?

Yes, they _____.

2 Look at 1. Write **Is** or **Are**. Then answer.

1 _____ she eating?

_____

2 _____ he reading?

_____

3 _____ they climbing?

_____

4 _____ they running?

_____

My BIG ENGLISH World

1

My name: _____

My age: _____

ME

FOLD

©2015 Pearson Education Ltd

ENGLISH
AROUND ME

Paste or draw things with English words.

MOVIE TICKET

My Favorite Unit:

My Favorite Words:
- stuffed animal
- hello • goodbye • pencil
- jumping rope • finger
- long • mom • pizza

1 Good Morning, Class!
2 My Family
3 My Body
4 My Favorite Clothes

FOLD

My Favorite Project:

How are you?

What's your favorite color?

5 Busy at Home
6 On the Farm
7 Party Time
8 Fun and Games
9 Play Time